**teach
yourself**

**beginner's arabic
script**
john mace

D1114291

For UK order enquiries: please contact Bookpoint Ltd, 130
Milton Park, Abingdon, Oxon OX14 4SB. Telephone: +44 (0)
1235 827720, Fax: +44 (0) 1235 400454. Lines are open
9.00–18.00, Monday to Saturday, with a 24-hour message
answering service. You can also order through our website
www.madaboutbooks.com.

For USA order enquiries: please contact McGraw-Hill Customer
Services, P.O. Box 545, Blacklick, OH 43004-0545, USA.
Telephone: 1-800-722-4726. Fax: 1-614-755-5645.

For Canada order enquiries: please contact McGraw-Hill
Ryerson Ltd, 300 Water St, Whitby, Ontario L1N 9B6, Canada.
Telephone: 905 430 5000. Fax: 905 430 5020.

Long renowned as the authoritative source for self-guided
learning – with more than 30 million copies sold worldwide – the
Teach Yourself series includes over 300 titles in the fields of
languages, crafts, hobbies, business, computing and education.

British Library Cataloguing in Publication Data: a catalogue entry
for this title is available from The British Library.

Library of Congress Catalog Card Number: On file

First published in UK 1999 by Hodder Headline Ltd, 338 Euston
Road, London, NW1 3BH.

First published in US 1999 by Contemporary Books, a Division
of The McGraw Hill Companies, 1 Prudential Plaza, 130 East
Randolph Street, Chicago, IL 60601 USA.

This edition published 2003.

The 'Teach Yourself' name is a registered trade mark of Hodder
& Stoughton Ltd.

Copyright © 1999, 2003 John Mace

Typeset by John Mace
Printed in Great Britain for Hodder & Stoughton Educational, a
division of Hodder Headline Ltd, 338 Euston Road, London NW1
3BH by Cox & Wyman Ltd, Reading, Berkshire.

Impression number   10 9 8 7 6 5 4 3 2 1
Year   2007 2006 2005 2004 2003

Acknowledgements

I am grateful to the following organisations for their kind permission to reproduce certain original material in this book:
- Shell International Ltd. for the line drawing of a road tanker shown on p. 55, taken from their publication 'Oil for Everybody',
- Al-Hayat newspaper for the three headlines shown on p. 123,
- the Bank of Lebanon for the banknote shown on p. 124.

I am also indebted to Marilyn Moore for her indefatigable proof-reading and checking. Any errors now found in this text are my responsibility.

Books on Arabic by the same author

Arabic Today, a student, business and professional course in spoken and written Arabic, Edinburgh University Press 1996, ISBN 0 7486 0616 5
Arabic Grammar, A Reference Guide, Edinburgh University Press 1998, ISBN 0 7486 1079 0
Teach Yourself Arabic Verbs and Essential Grammar, Hodder & Stoughton 1999, ISBN 0 340 73008 0

CONTENTS

INTRODUCTION

Reading and writing Arabic

Arabic writing seems daunting at first sight, but it doesn't have to be. This book attempts to take the mystique out of it. You learn the alphabet in stages, practising each new letter or combination of letters many times before moving on to the next; at the same time you fit the letters into useful words and phrases seen everywhere in any Arab environment.

This book is actual; you learn to read and write today's Arabic. And you learn through practice, from the start.

That said, nobody can promise that when you have finished this book you'll be able to read a newspaper article, or write a report. That requires a knowledge of Arabic grammar going beyond our immediate scope. But you will be able to read and understand important signs and directions - even better, you will know what sort of words to expect. You will also be able to read and understand many newspaper headlines, and to write everything you can read.

The Arabic language

Arabic is a world language. It is the official language, or one of the official languages, of nineteen countries spread across Saharan Africa and most of the Middle East. It is also one of the official languages of the United Nations. Arab culture has a high reputation, and is studied at countless universities in the western world.

Words in Arabic are built on a 'root' of three (occasionally four) consonants, which contain the basic idea underlying all the words made from the root. An example is the root consisting of the three consonants **k t b**, which has the basic idea of *writing*. From this root Arabic makes:

- the verb **katab** *to write*
- the noun **kātib** for *writer*
- **maktūb** for *written* or for *letter*
- **kitāba** for the action of *writing*
- **maktab** for *office*, or the place where one writes
- **kitāb** for *book*
- **maktaba** for *library* or *bookshop*, and so on.

The words may have bits added on, or may change internally, but you still find the three root consonants, all present and always in the same order, throughout all the derivatives.

This is of enormous help. It means that if you know one Arabic word of a particular root, you can make an intelligent guess at the meaning of a previously unknown word showing that root.

Spoken Arabic varies from place to place. It is not normally written down (there is not even an agreed way to spell it), and it is never used for formal or official written communication.

But written Arabic is the same throughout the Arab world. The Cairo newspaper **al-'ahrām** (*The Pyramids*) is read with ease in Casablanca, at the other end of North Africa. This is the Arabic found on all signs, notices, advertisements and so on, and it has a standard pronunciation. This is the form of Arabic which we are about to explore.

The Arabic alphabet

First, some essential principles on which the Arabic alphabet is based. Refer back here if you are in doubt later:

- ■ The writing runs from right to left ← ←.
- ■ There are no capital letters.
- ■ Short vowels (the sounds **a** as in English *man*, **i** as in English *pin*, and **u** as in English *put*) are mostly not written; we usually have to infer them from the context.
- ■ Printed Arabic is originally an imitation of handwriting. Most of the letters (called 'joined letters') are joined to the letter following them in the same word. A few letters ('disjoined letters') are never joined to the letter following them.

All this sounds complicated. It is not. Don't attempt to remember it now; it will become familiar as you read and write.

How to use this book

This is a participative book. You have to do a geat deal of reading and writing. You learn, and remember, by doing.

Arm yourself at the outset with a solid exercise book with lined paper. Do all your writing in this exercise book. You should also write out your vocabulary somewhere permanent, whether in the back of this exercise book, or in a different one. Writing is a powerful aid to memory.

Units 1 to 6: Alphabet

Follow the text, practising writing each new letter or group of letters as instructed. Pay attention to the notes on handwriting; there are certain important differences between handwriting and print. In the 'Read and write' parts of each unit, you see both. Imitate the handwriting for preference: you can write like printing if you wish, but it looks unnatural, and is slower. Read your writing back. Read and write everything several times.

The letters are taught in an order which helps you to build up quickly a battery of words which you can write. Any pitfalls are pointed out on the way. From letters you will move to words. Also in these units, your progress is monitored with a series of exercises at each stage; then at the end of the unit you have tests, which are more difficult than the exercises as they offer only the barest of help, and are more formal.

Don't move on to a new unit until you are at least reasonably confident about the last one - and that includes having performed well in the tests, for which you can check your answers in the key.

While following these units, don't force yourself to learn words by heart. Some will stick in your mind anyway - so much the better. The important thing is that you can by now put the letters together correctly, and decipher the written combinations which you see.

In Unit 6 you also learn to read and write the Arabic numerals.

Units 7 to 13: Words and Structures

In these units you learn to identify the different types of word, how to manipulate them, and how to link them in common and useful expressions and sentences. You will begin to read notices, signs, headlines. Units 9 to 13 start with new vocabulary, usually divided into 'essential' vocabulary, which you need to learn now because of its importance, and 'reference' vocabulary which is used for exercises and tests, but which you need not learn at this stage; examine it, and refer to it as you work through the unit. You will retain much of it through practice. In these units you will also learn related word-patterns which are a helpful feature of Arabic. These units also have exercises and tests.

Unit 14

This unit gives you some important geographical vocabulary for the Arab world, and a map.

Unit 15

Go carefully through the general reading test in this unit, checking your performance with the key and going back into the book where necessary.

Key to Tests

This is self-explanatory.

Vocabularies

The preamble to this section explains how to use these.

Index

The Index lists alphabetically all the technical topics covered (e.g. Construct, Noun, Participle), showing where each is found.

Pocket Card

This is found at the end of the book, and its use is explained there.

1

In this unit you will learn
- six common letters, with their pronunciation,
- when and how to join these letters,
- something about the 'stress' of a word,
- words which you can read and write, using the six letters.

General
Before starting this unit, be sure to read the Introduction; the section entitled 'The Arabic alphabet' is important for understanding the terms used below.

Letters
1

| ا alif |

The first and commonest letter of the alphabet is ا, called **alif**. It represents:

- at the beginning of a word: any of the *short* vowel sounds **a-, u-, i-** (like *a* in English *ant*, *u* in English *put*, and *i* in English *ink*, respectively).
- in the middle of a word, a *long* vowel sound **-ā-**. Imagine pronouncing *man*, in English, but drawing the vowel out: *ma-a-an*.
- at the end of a few words: short **-a**.

ا **alif** is a so-called 'disjoined' letter, that is, it is never joined to the following letter.

alif rests on the line of writing, but is 'tall' like a European *l*. Write this letter several times, starting at the right of the page: ....← ←

2

آ alif madda

alif with a stroke over it represents long **ā** (see paragraph 1 above) at the beginning of the word. This variant of **alif** is called **alif madda**.

Write this letter several times; first the downstroke, then the head:...← ←

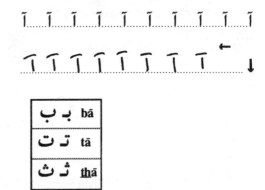

3

ب	بـ	**bā**
ت	تـ	**tā**
ث	ثـ	**th̲ā**

The sounds **b**, **t** and **th̲** (soft, like *th* in *think*; the transcription is underlined to show that it is a single sound) are written respectively with the letters called **bā**, **tā** and **th̲ā** (see paragraph 1 for the pronunciation of ā). These letters are all 'shallow', i.e. they all rest on the line of writing, and are not 'tall' like **alif**.

These are 'joined' letters, that is, they are joined to any letter following them in the same word. Each letter has two possible forms: the short form is used at the beginning or in the middle of a word, and the longer form (the 'full' form) when the letter stands at the end of the word, or alone.

You will note that the three letters are identical but for the dots. These are an integral part of the letter, just as they are in English *i* or *j*. The dot(s) lie over or under the beginning of the short form, and over or under the middle of the long form. In all dotted letters the stroke is written first (← right to left), then the dot or dots.

These are the printed and typed forms. In normal handwriting, two dots usually become a dash –, and three dots something like a circumflex accent ^. Write a line of each letter, first with the dots as in print, then as in normal handwriting.

Start at the right: .... ←←

We can now write a few words. ‎ا‎ is always written downwards except in
its middle form, i.e. when joined to a previous letter; then it is written
upwards. Remember that it is never joined to the following letter, that is,
to its left. Remember also, as was said in the Introduction, that short
middle and short final vowels are not normally written. Note the
difference in height between **alif** (tall) and **bā-tā-thā** (shallow).

Read and write (starting at the right, remember):   ←

آب ‎آب‎ **āb** *August*

اب ‎ا اب‎ **ab** *father**

باب ‎باب‎ **bāb** *door**

اثاث ‎اثاث‎ **athā́th** *furniture*

ثابت ‎ثا بت‎ **thā́bit** *firm, solid*

* There is no word for *a* or *an* in Arabic, so for example ‎اب‎ **ab** means
either *father* or *a father*, and ‎باب‎ **bāb** either *door* or *a door*.

Short vowel rule: *Short vowels (**a, i, u**) in the middle or at the end of
a word are not normally written. In a few words final **alif** is written
for short* **-a**.

---

4   Stress

Think of the English word *production*; its middle vowel *u* is pronounced
more strongly than the rest of the word. We say the *u* is *stressed*.

In books teaching English as a foreign language, the stress is sometimes marked with an accent (*prodúction*). We shall use this device in transcription in the first five units of this book: you see this in **atháth** and **thá**bit above.

Exercise 1 Match these words with their sound and their meaning given in the list below. The first one is done for you:

(a) اب **ab** *father*   (b) آب   (c) اثاث   (d) باب

atháth, āb, bāb; *door, furniture, August.*

Exercise 2 In Exercise 1, mark the **áli**fs which are pronounced long, **ā**.

Exercise 3 Write the word باب **bāb** *door*. Why is the first **bā** written differently from the last one? And why isn't the whole word joined up?

The answers to these exercises follow paragraph 6 below.

5

We write the sound **n** with the joined letter **nūn** (**n** as in English, long **ū** like *u* in English *truth*). This letter has a short form used at the beginning or in the middle of a word, and a full form used at the end of the word, or when the letter stands alone. The dot is an integral part of the letter. The short form differs from **bā** (paragraph 3 above) only in the position of the dot, while the full form starts just above the line of writing and swoops below it and up again. We can call it a 'deep' shape. In handwriting, the dot of full-form **nūn** often takes the form of a hook on the curve itself: ن

Write several examples of **nūn**, first as in print, i.e. with a dot on the full form; then with a hook on that form as in normal handwriting:..........←←

ن...........ن............نـ...........ن............نـ...........نـ

ن...........ن............ن...........نـ............ن...........ن

Now *read and write* more words with the five letters we know (from the right):...←←

ابن ابن **ibn** *son*   بنت بنت **bint** *daughter, girl*

انت ‫انتـ‬ **ánta** *you* ....   انا ‫انا‬ **ána** *I* ....

نبات ‫نبـات‬ **nabất** *vegetation* ....   بنات ‫بنات‬ **banất** *daughters* ....

Always *write* your words, don't draw or trace them. Don't grip the pen tightly, and think ahead about what you are writing, so that you anticipate which form of the coming letters you are going to use.

6

The 'joined' letter **yā** represents:

- ■ at the beginning of a word: the consonant **y-** (like English *y* in *year*).
- ■ in the middle of a word: either the consonant **-y-** (see above), or the long vowel **-ī-** (like *i* in English *machine*), or the vowel-combination **-ay-** (like *ay* in English *day*).
- ■ at the end of a word: the long vowel **-ī** (see above).

The letter **yā** is *never* pronounced like the vowel-sound *y* in English *my*.

Like the **bā-tā-thā** group which we learned earlier, this letter has a shallow short form used at the beginning or in the middle of a word, and a full form at the end if the word, or when the letter stands alone. The short form is identical to **tā** except that its two dots are below; its full form has a deep shape and is quite different, swooping below the line and up again. Write **yā** several times, first with dots and then in the handwritten form, with a dash:... ←←

‫يـ‬ .... ‫يـ‬ ‫يـ‬ .... ‫ي‬ ‫يـ‬ .... ‫ي‬ .... ‫يـ‬

‫يـ‬ .... ‫يـ‬ ‫يـ‬ .... ‫يـ‬ ‫يـ‬ .... ‫يـ‬ .... ‫يـ‬

More words. ***Read and write*** (remember that initial **yā** must be **y-**, middle **yā** can be **-y-**, **-ī-** or **-ay-**, while final **yā** is **-ī**):

بيت ‫بيت‬ **bayt** *house* ....   بيتين ‫بيتيـن‬ **baytáyn** *two houses* ....

اثنين اثنين‎ ithnáyn *two*   بنايات بنايات‎ bināyất *buildings*

بنتين بنتين‎ bintáyn *two daughters/girls*

In their short forms, the letters ـ ت ث ن ـ‎ are called 'toothed letters' -
the form ـ‎ is a 'tooth'.

When full-form ي‎ is preceded by one or more toothed letters, there are
special handwritten shapes, which you should always use even if they are
not present in print:

tooth + final ي‎: سي مى‎   *teeth + final* ي‎: سي مى‎

Read and write:

ابي ابي‎ ábī *my father*   بناتي بناتي‎ banấtī *my daughters*

ياباني ياباني‎ yābấnī *Japanese*   بنتي بنتي‎ bíntī *my daughter*

ابني ابني‎ íbnī *my son*   بيتي بيتي‎ báytī *my house*

(Remember to pronounce the stress on the vowel marked with an
accent: **ábī**.)

Exercise 4 Match each of the following words with its sound and its
meaning. The first one is done for you:

(a) بيت‎ **bayt** *house*   (b) بنتي‎   (c) بنايات‎   (d) ابني‎
        bināyất, bíntī, íbnī; *buildings, my son, my daughter.*

Exercise 5 Write all the Arabic words you know which (a) begin with
ا‎ or آ‎, or (b) end in ي‎, or (c) have ن‎ in them. Expressions with the
additional meaning *my* or *two* do not count.

The answers to these exercises are given after this paragraph.

You will recall that ـي...‎ yā at the beginning of the word gives the sound
y-. We also know that initial ...ا‎ álif represents a short initial vowel. Note
now that any word beginning with a *long* vowel or a vowel-
combination in pronunciation must be introduced in writing by álif,
which itself then has no sound. So initial ī- or ay- is written ...ايـ‎ (the álif

being silent). *Read and write:*

اين اين ..... áyna *where*

Initial long vowel rule: *Any long vowel or vowel-combination beginning a word must be introduced by* **álif** *in writing; the* **álif** *itself is then not pronounced.*

Answers to Exercises

Exercise 1 (b) آب āb *August;* (c) اثاث aṯẖáṯẖ *furniture;* (d) باب bāb *door.*

Exercise 2 The words are are آب , اثاث and باب. The other **álif**s are short, pronounced **a**.

Exercise 3 The letter ب ب bā has the long form at the end of the word, and the short form at the beginning or in the middle. And the word isn't joined up completely because it has to break after ا **álif** which is never joined to the next letter, i.e. it is a *disjoined* letter.

Exercise 4 (b) بنتي bíntī *my daughter* (c) بنايات bināyāt *buildings* (d) ابني íbnī *my son.*

Exercise 5 The total list studied so far (in order of appearance) is:

(a) آب اب اثاث ابن انت انا اثنين اين   (b) ياباني

(c) بنت ابن انت انا نبات بنات اثنين ياباني اين

If you got more than 12 out of the whole 18, you did well. If you scored below 9, it would be a good idea to re-read the unit and note what you missed.

Tests

1   Write the letters as a word. For example, (a) ب ي ت is بيت :

(a) ب ي ت   (b) ب ي ت ي ن   (c) ا ب ن ي
(d) ا ث ا ث ي   (e) ن ب ا ت

2   Read aloud your handwritten answers to Test 1. For example, (a) is **bayt**.

3   Read aloud. For example, (a) is **banāt**:

(c) ياباني   (b) اثنين   (a) بنات

(e) ابني   (d) اين

4   Write. For example, (a) is أبني :
   (a) **ibnī**   (b) **bintayn**   (c) **bināyātī**
   (d) **bābayn**   (e) **ayna**   (f) **a<u>th</u>ā<u>th</u>ī**

5   Read the words. What is the sound of each ا in each example?
     Explain why. For example, in (a) ابن **ibn** it is **i**, because here ا stands
     for the short vowel **i**:

(c) آب   (b) باب   (a) ابن

(e) اثنين   (d) نبات

Review

In this unit we studied six letters (plus one variant), five of them extremely common. You learned

- that **álif** at the beginning or a word either stands for a *short* vowel (**a, i, u**) or introduces a *long* vowel **ī** or a *vowel-combination* **ay**,
- that **álif mádda** always represents long **ā**,
- the important difference between short and long vowels,
- that short vowels (**a, i, u**) in the middle or at the end of a word are not usually written, though final **álif** sometimes expresses short **-a**,
- the important difference between 'joined' and 'disjoined' letters,
- the difference between 'tall', 'shallow' and 'deep' written shapes,
- all the 'toothed' letters, including how to write final **yā** after a tooth and after teeth.

You have practised reading and writing joined letters (ي , ن , ث , ت , ب) in full and short forms, also taking account of tall, shallow and deep shapes.

You have read and written 22 different words out of many more which are now within your grasp.

There is a lot in this first unit; that is because with any fewer than these six letters you would get fewer than ten words, and who wants that? You have made your first encounter with this writing system which is totally different from that of any European language; don't be surprised or discouraged if it looks tough. Go back and read through the unit again, and pick up anything that baffled you the first time. Don't look for immediate perfection. Keep going; things will get clearer, and you will gain confidence, as we advance.

2

In this unit you will learn

- three more letters, also very common, with their pronunciation,
- words which you can read and write, using these letters,
- how to write doubled letters,
- how to express *the*.

Letters
1

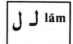

The letter called **lām** represents the sound *l*. Pronounce it *light*, as in English *leaf*, not *dark* as in *wall*. **lām** looks like a European handwritten *l* written in the opposite direction. **lām** is a joined* letter; the short and full forms are used exactly like those of any other joined letter, e.g. ﺑ ﺏ **bā** which we already know. However, both forms of **lām** are tall*, while the full form is also deep*, with a swoop.

* Look again at Unit 1 for the meaning of these terms, if you are unsure.

Write this letter several times: short form tall, full form both tall and deep:

| ل | ﻟ | ل | ﻟ | ل | ﻟ |
| ﻟ | ﺭ | ﻟ | ﺝ | ﺝ | ﻟ |

You might think that **álif** and the short form of **lām** get confused; in practice this is not so. **álif** is disjoined, **lām** is joined, and there is never confusion. Look, for example, at <u>**thá**lith</u> *'third'* below. Read and write:

ﺛﺎﻟﺚ ﺛﺎﻟﺚ	<u>thá</u>lith *third*	ﻟﻲ ﻟﻲ	**lī** *to me, for me*
ﻟﺒﻨﺎﻧﻲ ﻟﺒﻨﺎﻧﻲ	**lubnānī** *Lebanese*	ﻟﺒﻨﺎﻥ ﻟﺒﻨﺎﻥ	**lubnán** *Lebanon*
		ﺍﺑﻞ ﺍﺑﻞ	**íbil** *camels*

The combination **lām** + **álif** has special forms. In print and type, the **álif** is sloped and joins the **lām** at the latter's middle. In handwriting, we *break* the joint, and may either slope the **álif** or leave it upright. In both cases, the **álif** is written *downwards*. Look at the following forms:

	handwriting	*print and type*
not following a joined letter	لا لا	لا
following a joined letter	لـ لـ	لـ

Imitate one of the handwritten forms in each case.

Read and write (choose which form you prefer):

.... ثلاث ثلاث **thaláth** *three* .... آلات آلات **álát** *tools*

.... لا **la** *no*

You will never see the form (لـ) in correctly written Arabic, whether in handwriting or print.

The break in the connection of **lám-álif** in handwriting does not mean that the **lám** has suddenly become a disjoined letter; it is merely a peculiarity of handwritten style.

2

م مـ **mím**

The sound **m** (as in English *me*) is written with the letter called **mím**. This letter is joined. Its two forms are used exactly as are the two forms of the other joined letters. Its short form is shallow, while the full form is deep with a straight downward tail. The 'bead' of both forms rests on the line of writing.

When **mim** is not joined to a preceding letter (i.e. to its right), its bead can be written clockwise or anticlockwise. Write this letter several times:

Read and write (the bead can go either way round):

.... من من **min** *from* .... امام امام **amám** *in front of*

But when joined to a preceding letter, the **mim** is approached from the top, and written *anticlockwise* ↻. This gives us special combinations after certain letters, which may or may not be used in print, but which are *always* used in handwriting. Write the handwritten forms:

	handwriting		*print and type*	
tooth + mīm	م	ﻤ	نم	ﻨﻤ\نم
teeth + mīm	ﻤ	ﻨﻤ	ننم	ﻨﻨﻤ\ننم
lām + mīm	لم	ﻠﻤ	لم	ﻠﻤ\لم
mīm + mīm	م	ﻤ	مم	ﻤﻤ\مم

Now *read and write:*

تمام........تمام tamám *perfect*   نمل........نمل naml *ants*

الماني الماني....... almáni *German*   انتم........انتم ántum *you*

Exercise 1 Match these words with their sound and their meaning given in the list below. The first one is done for you:

(a) الماني almáni *German* (b) تمام (c) ثالث (d) ثلاث
tháli**th**, **th**alá**th**, tamám; *perfect, third, three.*

Exercise 2 Complete the word with the right form of **lām-álif**:

no ... (c)   آ...ت (b)   ث..ث (a)

Exercise 3 The consul has got the nationalities mixed. Sort them out:

(a) الماني (b) ياباني (c) لبناني (d) ليبي
Japanese, Lebanese, Libyan, German; **almá**nī, **lí**bī, **yābá**nī, **lubná**nī
(One of these words is new, but you can handle it.)

The answers to these exercises follow paragraph 5 below.

3

و **wow**

The letter called **wow** is deep and disjoined (you know what that means now). It has only one form, with a half-swoop downwards and along only, not up. Write it several times, starting with the ring written *clockwise* and resting on the line of writing:

و........و........و.......و.......و.......و...........

و............و.......و........و........و...........

The letter **wow** represents the following sounds:

- at the beginning of a word: the consonant **w-** (like *w* in English *weak*).
- in the middle of a word: either the consonant **-w-** (see above), or the long vowel **-ū-** (like *u* in English *truth*), or the vowel-combinations **-ou-** (as in English *soul**) or **-ow-** (as in English *now*).
- at the end of a word: the long vowel **-ū** (see above) or, in a few words, **-ow** (see above).

The letter **wow** is *never* pronounced like *u* in English *union*.

* The pronounciation **ou** is not officially correct; the vowel-combination should sound **ow**. But in certain words even educated Arabs read it aloud as **ou** except in very formal circumstances. We shall show it as it sounds in ordinary reading aloud.

Look back to Unit 1, paragraph 6, the description of **yā**, very similar to the description given above for **wow**. Both letters are used to represent a consonant, or a long vowel, or a vowel-combination, in corresponding positions.

Read and write (remember that initial **wow** must be **w-**, middle **wow** can be **-w-**, **-ū-**, **-ou-** or **-ow-**, and final **wow** is **-ū-** or, less often, **-ow-**):

ثانوي ثَانَوِي	**thânawī** *secondary*	و.........و.........	**wa** *and*
يوم يَوْم	**youm** *day*	لون لَوْن	**loun** *colour*
يوليو يُولِيو	**yūliyū** *July*	يونيو يُونِيو	**yūniyū** *June*
ممنون مَمْنُون	**mamnūn** *grateful*	بيوت بِيُوت	**buyūt** *houses*
مايو مَايُو	**mâyū** *May*	تمويل تَمْوِيل	**tamwīl** *financing*

Also back in Unit 1, paragraph 6, we recorded the fact that any word beginning with a *long* vowel or a vowel-*combination* in pronunciation must be introduced in writing by **álif**, which itself then has no sound. This applies to the sounds **ū-**, **ou-** and **ow-** beginning a word: all these sounds in this situation are written أو... (the **alif** being silent).

Read and write:

او..او..... **ow** *or*

4 Doubled Letters

When we have two identical letters separated by a vowel (long or short), then we write both letters: in the word ممنون *grateful* (shown above) we have two examples: (**m** + *short vowel* + **m**) and (**n** + *long vowel* + **n**). Whether the vowel is short and unwritten or long and written makes no difference; there is a vowel, and the two identical letters are shown.

But when we have a *doubled letter*, i.e. two identical letters with *no* intervening vowel, we write only one letter. *Read and write:*

ممثل..... **mumáththil** *representative*   اول..اول... **áwwal** *first*

> **Doubled Letter Rule.** *Letters which are sounded double (i.e. with no intervening vowel) are written single.*

Although we write the doubled letter single, it is most important to *pronounce* it doubled, i.e. *hold* it for longer than normal. Imagine saying *butter* as *but-ter*. The two words shown above then sound as if they were transcribed **áw-wal** and **mumáth-thil**. This is the correct pronunciation.

Think of the double *-nn-* in *innumerable*. If you know Italian, you have no problem; think of the double *-tt-* in *città*.

There is a way of showing doubled letters in script. It is the sign called

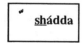

ُ **shádda**

This sign, which is not a letter of the alphabet, can be written above any letter to show that it is doubled. I say 'can be' as it is often left out; but since **shádda** is so useful we shall use it for the rest of this book. You should always write it where appropriate.

Read and write, distinguishing single letters from doubled:

لَمّا ... لَا lámma *when* .... لمن لِمَنْ li-man *whose*

مُمَثّل ... مُمَثّل mumáth̲th̲il *representative* .... مثل مِثْل mith̲l *like*

تلال ... تِلال tilál *hills* .... تَلّ تَلّ tall *hill*

Exercise 4 Put **shadda** wherever appropriate, and pronounce the word. The first one is done:

مُمَثّل (a) mumáth̲th̲il تمويل (b) اول (c) ممنون (d)

Give the meaning of each word. The first is *representative*.

The answers to this exercise follow paragraph 5 below.

5 Definite Article - *The*

The important word *the* is called the *definite article*, or more simply the *article*. We use it before a *noun* (i.e. a word denoting a person, place, thing or idea). In Arabic, it takes the form الـ... **al-**, which is always attached to the word which it 'defines', i.e. makes definite. We show it with a hyphen; you should pronounce the whole thing as one word.

Read and write:

البيت .... البيت **al-bayt** *the house*

البنات .... البنات **al-banát** *the daughters*

The article is used in Arabic more often than is *the* in English; it is especially common with geographical terms, and with words used in a general or universal meaning.

Read and write these examples:

اليابان .... اليابان **al-yābán** (*'the'*) *Japan*

الموت .... الموت **al-mowt** (*'the'*) *death* (i.e. in general)

al- is its normal pronunciation. But when the defined word begins with a sound pronounced with the tip or near-tip of the tongue, the **l** merges with (the technical term is 'assimilates to') that sound, producing a doubled sound. The spelling stays the same. Look carefully first at the spelling and pronunciation of the following expressions, then *read and write* them. We show the doubled letter with <u>shádda</u>:

التَّلّ .... التَّلّ   **at-tall** (not *al-...*) *the hill*

التِّلال .... التِّلال   **at-tilál** *the hills*

النِّيل .... النِّيل   **an-níl** *the Nile*

الثَّالث .... الثَّالث   **a<u>th</u>-<u>th</u>á**lith *the third one*

اللون .... اللون*   **al-loun** *the colour*

اللبناني .... اللبناني*   **al-lubnáni** *the Lebanese (person)*

There are fourteen letters which have this effect on the l of the article. So far we have learned four of them: ت , ث , ن and ل . The fourteen letters concerned are called by the Arabs 'sun letters'. We shall point out the remaining ten sun letters as we meet them. The important thing to remember is that in such words we pronounce as double the first letter of the defined word, dropping the l of the article in pronunciation but not in spelling.

* Two letters l written together, even though there is no intervening vowel. This is an exception to the rule about doubled letters.

You will also have noticed that the article ...الـ never affects the stress of the word, and never takes the stress itself.

One final note: the ...الـ of الماني *German* is not the article; it is part of the word itself. We learn in Unit 3 how to add the article to a word like this.

Exercise 5 Make each word definite with the article. Write your answer, then match it with the transcription and the meaning. The first one is done:

(a) بيت → البيت al-**bayt** *the house* (b) ممثّل (c) تمويل (d) نبات
an-nabát, at-tamwíl, al-mumá<u>ththi</u>l; *(the) financing,*
the representative, the vegetation.

Exercise 6 In your answers to Exercise 5, underline the articles whose l assimilates to a sun letter at the beginning of the defined word.

Exercise 7 Why are ا ، ب ، ي ، م and و so-called 'moon' letters, i.e. not sun letters? (Pronounce them, and you will see - or rather, feel - why.)

The answers to these exercises are immediately below.

Answers to Exercises

Exercise 1 (b) تمام tamám *perfect* (c) ثالث thálith *third*
(d) ثلاث thaláth *three*

Exercise 2 (a) ثلاث (b) آلات (c) لا

Exercise 3 (a) الماني almáni *German* (b) ياباني yābáni *Japanese*
(c) لبناني lubnáni *Lebanese* (d) ليبي líbi *Libyan*

Exercise 4 (a) ممثّل mumáththil *representative* (b) تمويل tamwíl *financing,* (c) اوّل áwwal *first,* (d) ممنون mamnún *grateful*

Exercise 5 (b) الممثّل al-mumáththil *the representative* (b) التمويل at-tamwíl *(the) financing* (d) النّبات an-nabát *the vegetation*

Exercise 6 (c) التمويل (d) النّبات

Exercise 7 Because they are not pronounced with the tip or near-tip of the tongue.

Tests

1 Write the letters as a word. For example, (a) ال ن ي ل is النّيل :
   (a) ال ن ي ل   (b) ال ت م و ي ل   (c) ا و ل
   (d) ال م ا ن ي   (e) م م ن و ن

2 Read aloud your handwritten answers to Test 1. For example, (a) is **an-níl**.

3 Read aloud. For example, (a) is **lubnáni**:
   (a) لبناني   (b) اوّل   (c) الثالث
   (d) ممنون   (e) النمل

4   Write. For example, (a) is اللِّيبي :

   (a) **al-líbī**   (b) **muma<u>th</u>thiláyn**   (c) **at-tamwíl**

   (d) **an-níláyn***   (e) **ow**   (f) **al-yābā́nī**

   (* i.e. two, the Blue and the White. They meet at Khartoum.)

5   In the following list, the words اب\البنات\ابن form a group as
   they all denote family relationships. Assemble the other logical
   groups, and say why their words belong together:

ابن، الماني، الثالث، البنات، يونيو، البيوت، اب، اول،
ياباني، لبناني، يوليو، البنايات، اثنين، ثلاث، آب، ليبي،
مايو.

Review

In this Unit we studied three common letters and one special sign
called <u>sh</u>ádda. You learned also

■ how to read and write the special forms of **lām-álif**,

■ how to join the letter **mīm**,

■ how to write doubled letters,

■ how to express the article *the*, and how to pronounce it,

You have had more practice with tall, shallow and deep shapes.

Hopefully you have also become a little more fluent in reading and
writing, and you probably now find writing 'the other way round'
less strange.

3

In this unit you will learn

- a very important non-alphabetical sign,
- more about the article *the*,
- three more letters, plus one variant, with their pronunciation,
- more words,
- how to make 'feminine' words.

hámza

1 Listen to someone say emphatically: 'absolutely awful'. You will hear a catch of the breath before each of the *a*'s. We could represent it with an apostrophe: *'absolutely 'awful*.

This is called a 'glottal stop', the glottis being that part of the throat which stops or releases breath when we speak. The stop is written in Arabic with a non-alphabetical sign called **hámza**:

> **ء** hámza

hámza is never joined to anything. Write it several times:

.............ء ....ء ....ء ....ء ....ء

.............ء ....ء ....ء ....ء ....ء

Its form is simple enough, but it is used in many ways. You will see it in the following guises:

- above or below **álif**: أ إ ,
- above **wow**, or **yā** *without its dots*: 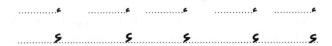 ؤ ئ ئ ,
- standing alone, on or near the line of writing: ء .

Whole chapters have been written about the correct writing of **hámza**. For our purposes, it is sufficient if we learn to pronounce the glottal stop whenever we see the sign ء. We transcribe it with an apostrophe: ' .

Many Arabic words apparently beginning with a vowel, such as **ab**, in fact begin with a glottal stop. The writing often marks it with **hámza**, but it is equally often ignored.

For clarity, from now on in this book we shall show initial **hámza** on the Arabic of all words which have it, thus: أب . We shall continue to transcribe without the apostrophe.

You should continue to write without initial **hámza**; that is always acceptable.

In the middle or at the end of a word, however, the **hámza** is always written, and you should write it, too.

One last point: آ **álif mádda** is deemed to have an 'in-built' **hámza**, so while the stop is pronounced, no 'further' **hámza** is written.

Read and write:

أنباء انباء anbá' *news (items)* .... نبأ نبأ **nába'** *news item*

نائم نائم **ná'im** *asleep* .... الآن الآن **'al-'ān** *now*

تنبّؤ تنبّؤ **tanábbu'** *forecast* .... ثنائي ثنائي **thuná'ī** *double*

Definite Article (continued)

2   In Unit 2 we learned the article ...الـ : النيل، البيت .

When we attach the article to a word beginning with **hámza**, the **hámza** has to be written (unless we have **álif mádda**, in which the **hámza** is already present). We can leave out the **hámza** at the beginning of a word, but not once an article is added, since the **hámza** is now in the middle of the word. The article itself has no **hámza**.

Read and write:

الأب الأب **al-'ab** *the father* .... أب اب *father*

الإبل الإبل **al-'ibil** *the camels* .... إبل ابل *camels*

الأنباء الأنباء **al-'anbá'** *the news items* .... أنباء انباء *news items*

الآلات الآلات **al-'ālát** *the tools* .... آلات آلات *tools*

Some words begin with vowels which are deemed to have no stop, i.e. no **hámza**. *Read and write* the two already known to us:

......الابن ...الابن الابن **al-ibn** *the son* ....ابن ...ابن ابن *son*

.....الاثنين ...الاثنين الاثنين **al-ithnayn** *the two* ....اثنين ...اثنين اثنين *two*

Words of one letter

3   A few important words consist of one letter. *Read and write:*

...ل...ل ل **li** *to, for* .....ب...ب ب **bi** *with, by, in* .....و...و و **wa** *and*

It is a rule that one-letter words are written as part of the next word, e.g.:

........لبنات لبنات **li-banát** *for girls* ....وأنا...وأنا **wa-'ána** *and I*

which we transcribe with a hyphen for clarity. The article ...الـ itself does not begin with a **hámza** but with a so-called 'weak' vowel, that is, a vowel which is dropped when another vowel precedes it. This happens when a one-letter word is added to the article.

Read and write:

...............باليابان ...باليابان باليابان **bi-l-yában** (not *bi-al-*) *in Japan*

.................والنّيل ...والنّيل والنّيل **wa-n-níl** *and the Nile*

When the word ل (see above) is added to the article, the **álif** of the article is dropped in writing too:

...........للبنات ...للبنات للبنات **li-l-banát** *to/for (the) girls*

...........للتّمويل ...للتّمويل للتّمويل **li-t-tamwíl** *for (the) financing*

We do not, however, write more than two consecutive identical letters, even when the expression seems to demand more. Read and write:

...........للبناني ...للبناني للبناني **li-l-lubnáni** *for the Lebanese (man)*

Exercise 1 Write these words with the definite article, and pronounce them:

(a) الماني (b) إبل (c) أنباء (d) أب (e) أوّل

Fit the meanings to your answers: *the first, the news, the camels, the German, the father.*

Exercise 2 Add ل to your answers to Exercise 1 in writing. Give the meaning. Then fit the pronunciation to your answers:

li-l-'anbá', li-l-'ab, li-l-'almắnī, li-l-'áwwal, li-l-'ibil.

The answers to these exercises follow paragraph 6 below.

Letters
4

ه	ـه	ـه	ـحـ	ـهـ	هـ	hā

By far the most complicated letter in this alphabet, **hā** represents the sound *h* (as in English *he*). The **h** is sounded wherever you see the letter, even at the end of a word, unlike English. **hā** is a joined letter, shallow except in one case, with several possible forms:

- ◼ ـه at the beginning of a word or after a disjoined letter,
- ◼ *ـحـ or ـهـ in the middle of a word after a joined letter,
- ◼ ـه or *ـه at the end of a word after a joined letter,
- ◼ ه at the end of a word after a disjoined letter, or when standing alone.

* The middle form ـحـ is little used in handwriting, and the final form ـه is not used in print or typing.

Let us take this letter in stages. Everything rests on the line of writing except for the downward tick of ـحـ . Write first several initial letters **hā**:

Now the handwritten middle form:

Then the two final forms, both used in handwriting:

And finally the 'isolated' form:

Now *read and write*:

هي حمي	híya *she*	هو حمو	húwa *he*
هام حامّ	hámm *important*	هم حم	hum *they*
اهتمام اهتمام	ihtimám *attention*	نهائي نهائي	nihá'i *final*
تنبيه تنبيه	tanbíh *warning*	انتباه انتباه	intibáh *caution*
تمهّل تمهّل	tamáhhal *SLOW DOWN* (road sign)		

One important word with **hā** is spelt irregularly. Note: الله **alláh** *God*.

5

ة ـة ـة	**tā marbúṭa**

This one is a 'curiosity'. It is not an alphabetical letter, but final **hā** with the two dots of **tā**, and it is called **tā marbúṭa***, which means 'bound **tā**'. It is found only at the end of words, and is commonly used to make certain words 'feminine'. After a consonant, it has the sound **-a**; combined with ـ **ī** it gives the combination ـية... **-íya**. In handwriting the dots of **ة** are frequently left off; in print, never.

* The name of this letter itself contains a letter (**ṭ**) which we have not yet studied. No panic. We shall learn it properly the next time it occurs.

Read and write, comparing the 'masculine' ('m.') and 'feminine' ('f.') forms of words known to you:

grateful:	.............................ممنون	(m., of a man or boy)
	.... ممنونة	**mamnúna** (f., of a woman or girl)

important:	.... هامّة **hámma** (f.)	.... هامّ	(m.)
third:	.... ثالثة **thálitha** (f.)	.... ثالث	(m.)
Japanese:	.... يابانية **yābāníya** (f.)	.... ياباني	(m.)
German:	.... ألمانية **almāníya** (f.)	.... ألماني	(m.)
Lebanese:	.... لبنانية **lubnāníya** (f.)	...............لبناني	(m.)

The ending -**íya** carries the stress of the word, as shown.

Exercise 3 Match these words with their sound and their meaning given in the list below. The first one is done for you:

(a) ثنائي **thuna'í** *double*   (b)ممنونة   (c)ليبية   (d) اهتمام
      mamnúna, ihtimám, líbíya; *attention, grateful, Libyan.*

Exercise 4 Complete the word with the right handwritten form of **hā**:

(a) نـ..ائي   (b) ..و   (c) ...انتبا   (d) ...امّ   (e) ..سي

Read your answers aloud.

Exercise 5 Feminine (f.) or masculine (m.)?:

(a) ألماني   (b) ممنونة   (c) هي   (d) هامّ   (e) لبنانية

Read each word aloud.

The answers to these exercises follow paragraph 6 below.

6

The letters called **sīn** and **shīn** represent the sounds *s* (as in English *see*) and *sh* (as in English *she*) respectively. These are joined letters; the short and full forms are used like the short and full forms of ب . Short-form **sīn** and **shīn** are shallow and rest on the line of writing. The full form has a deep swoop. The two letters differ only in the dots, which are always situated as shown.

Despite appearances, these are not toothed letters (Unit 1, paragraph 6). In handwriting, we usually 'iron out' the indentations of these letters into a shallow curve, thus: س ڛ

Write several examples of each letter, first with indentations and printed dots, then with a curve and the dots run together into a circumflex (see Unit 1, paragraph 3):

sīn and <u>sh</u>īn are sun letters, so the ل of the article assimilates: **as-**, **a<u>sh</u>-**.

Read and write:

السّنة الـتـنه   **as-sana** *the year* ....   سنة ....ـنـة.... **sana** *year*

الاسم الاسم   **al-ism** *the name* ....   اسم اسم.... **ism** *name*

الأساس الأساس   **al-'asās** *the basis* ....   أساس اساس.... **asās** *basis*

شاي شاي   **<u>sh</u>āy** *tea* ....   شيء شيء.... **<u>sh</u>ay'** *thing*

الشّمس التّمس   **a<u>sh</u>-<u>sh</u>ams** *the sun* ....   شمس شمس.... **<u>sh</u>ams** *sun*

شمالي شمالي   **<u>sh</u>imālī** *northern* ....   شمال شمال.... **<u>sh</u>imāl** *north*

سؤال سؤال   **su'āl** *question* .... مسؤول مسؤول **mas'ūl** *responsible*

تأسيس يأسيس   **ta'sīs** *foundation* (the action) ....

التأسيس التأسيس   **at-ta'sīs** *the foundation* ....

ملابس ملابس   **malābis** *clothes* ....

Exercise 6 Read aloud the following signs and announcements:

(c) ملابس للبنات   (b) انتباه!   (a) بيت بالأثاث

What do they mean?

The answers to this exercise
are immediately below.

(d)

تمهّل

Answers to Exercises

Exercise 1 (a) الألماني al-'almánī *the German*

(b) الإبل al-'íbil *the camels*   (c) الأنباء al-'anbá' *the news*

(d) الأب al-'ab *the father*   (e) الأوّل al-'áwwal *the first*

Exercise 2 (a) للألماني li-l-'almánī *for the German*

(b) للإبل li-l-'íbil *for the camels*   (c) للأنباء li-l-'anbá' *for the news*

(d) للأب li-l-'ab *for the father*   (e) للأوّل li-l-'áwwal *for the first*

Exercise 3 (b) mamnúna *grateful* (c) lībíya *Libyan*
(d) ihtimám *attention*

Exercise 4 (a) نهائي nihá'ī (b) هو húwa (c) انتباه intibāh
(d) هامّ hāmm (e) هي híya

Exercise 5 (a) almánī m. (b) mamnúna f. (c) híya f. (d) hāmm m.
(e) lubnāníya f.

Exercise 6 (a) bayt bi-l-'atháth *House with Furniture*
(b) intibáh! *CAUTION!*   (c) malábis li-l-banát *Clothes for Girls*
(d) tamáhhal *SLOW DOWN*

Tests

1   Write the letters as a word. For example, (a) ش م س is شمس :
(a) ش م س   (b) ال ا س م   (c) ال م م ث ث ل
(d) أ ن ب ا ء   (e) ث ن ا ء ي

2 Read aloud your handwritten answers to Test 1. For example, (a) is <u>sh</u>ams.

3 Read aloud. For example, (a) is **al-ihtimám**:

(a) الاهتمام   (b) اللبنانية   (c) الألمانية

(d) بالأوّل   (e) بالثالثة

4 Put into the masculine form. For example, (a) is ممنون :

(a) ممنونة   (b) يابانية   (c) اللبنانية

(d) مسؤولة   (e) للثالثة

5 Pronounce your answers to Test 4. For example, (a) is **mamnún**.

6 In the last three units you have read and written all the following words. Fill in the missing letter in each one, in the right form. The first is نـ , making لبنانية:

(a) لبـ..انية   (b) ا...تـمام   (c) الملابـ...

(d) البـ..وت   (e) ثانـ..ي

If you have difficulty, you will find word (a) in paragraph 5 above, (b) in paragraph 4 above, (c) in paragraph 6 above (without its article), and (d) and (e) in Unit 2, paragraph 3.

Review

In this unit we studied three common letters, one variant, and the important sign called **hámza**. We also finished the article **al-** and its variants; you can now make definite any noun you know.

In this unit you also learned about feminine words and one-letter words. Your vocabulary now begins to expand spontaneously.

Finally, you have read four signs with authentic Arabic wording, using your knowledge under 'field' conditions.

4

In this unit you will learn
- six more letters, all of them sun letters,
- about 'dark' sounds,
- how to make common 'relative' words.

Letters
1

The letters called **rā** and **zayy** represent respectively *r* (which is always *rolled*, wherever it occurs) and *z* as in English *zoo*. These are *sun* letters, and are *disjoined*. The only difference in their appearance is the dot on **zayy**.

They are deep letters, written just like و **wow**, but without the ring, i.e. they start just above or at the line of writing, and make a half-swoop down and a little leftwards, but not up again. Write several:

These letters are joined to the previous letter in the normal way, except that, in handwriting, when they follow a tooth which is itself preceded by a letter, they have a special connection. Write the handwritten forms for **rā** (**zayy** is exactly the same, with a dot), paying special attention to the connection:

tooth + *tooth* + **r**	سـبـر......
m + *tooth* + **r**	مـصـر......
l + *tooth* + *r*	لـلـر......
s + *tooth* + **r**	سـسـر......

The short vowel **a** and the long vowel **ā**, when next to **rā**, are almost always 'darkened' in sound; the **a** sounds more like *u* in Southern English *but*, and the **ā** sounds more like the *a* of English *calm*. You will certainly notice it when you hear Arabs speak. Imitate it if you can; it is however not wrong or unintelligible if you don't.

In the list given below, 'dark' **a** and **ā** are shown as **ạ** and **ạ̄**, to help you.

Read and write:

مسرور	**masrúr** *pleased*	مرور	**murúr** *traffic*
متر	**mitr** *metre*	مرّة	**márra** *a time*
ليرة	**líra** *lira*	لتر	**litr** *litre*
الرّيال الرّيال	**ạr-riyál**	ريال	**riyál** *rial, riyal*
الرّئيس الرّئيس	**ạr-rạ̃́ĩs**	رئيس	**rạ̃́ĩs** *chairman**
الزّيارة الزّيارة	**az-ziyá̱ra**	زيارة	**ziyá̱ra** *visit*
شهر	**shahr** *month*	إيران	**īrá̱n** *Iran*
سيّارة	**sayyá̱ra** *car*	وزارة	**wizá̱ra** *ministry*

* also *chief, president, head* (person)

2

د **dāl**
ذ **dhāl**

These two letters, called **dāl** and **dhāl**, represent respectively *d* as in English *day* and hard *th* as in English *that*. Don't confuse this last sound with the soft *th* of ث **thā** (*think*), for which see Unit 1, paragraph 3.

These are both sun letters, and are disjoined. The only difference in their appearance is the dot on **dhāl**.

At first it seems they might be confused with **rā** and **zayy**. But there are important differences: ذ د are shallow, resting on the line of writing, and are always joined at the 'elbow'; ر ز are deep, and always joined at the head. Write several examples of **dāl** and **dhāl**:

د......ذ......ذ......د......ذ......ذ......د......ذ

د......ذ......ذ......د......ذ......ذ......د......ذ

Read and write:

الإدارة الإداره   **al-'idára**   إداره......   **idára** إدارة *administration*

الدّراسة الدّراس   **ad-dirása**   دراس......   **dirása** دراسة *study*

الدائرة الدائره   **ad-dá'ira**   دائره......   **dá'ira** دائرة *directorate*

مدير......   **mudír** *director*   مدرس......   **mádrasa** مدرسة *school*

الأستاذ الأستاذ   **al-'ustádh**   استاذ......   **ustádh** أستاذ *professor*

الابتداء الابتداء   **al-ibtidá'**   ابتداء......   **ibtidá'** ابتداء *beginning*

سيدة سيّده   **sayyida** *lady; Mrs*   سيّد......   **sayyid** سيّد *gentleman; Mr*

Exercise 1 Whose are these office doors? Read out their titles in Arabic and English:

| (d) الأستاذ | (c) الممثّل | (b) الرئيس | (a) المدير |

The answers to this exercise follow paragraph 4 below.

3

ṣād	صـ ص
ḍād	ضـ ض

Dark sounds

These two letters represent 'dark' sounds.

Think of the familiar sound *s*, represented by سين sīn (Unit 3). In pronouncing it, the tongue is high, following the curve of the palate. Now say *s* again, but this time dropping your tongue as low as possible, making a cavity at the bottom of the mouth. The *s* which you pronounce in this manner is 'dark'. It is ṣ, which is the sound of the letter ṣād.

Similarly, ḍ is a *d* said with low tongue, forming a cavity. It is the dark equivalent of the more familiar **d** of دال dāl (paragraph 2 above).

An immortal Australian writer once said his countrymen enjoy 'sin in the sun'. Think of the two *s*'s in this phrase, and the idea of light and dark letters seems less strange.

So much for the sounds. As to the shapes, ṣād and ḍād are both written identically except for the dot. They are joined, sun letters. The short form is shallow, resting on the line. Also, immediately after the loop it has a built-in tooth, which is never left out. The full form is deep, with a swoop. Write several:

Because of the tooth of short-form ṣād/ḍād, there are special connections in handwriting for ṣ/ḍ + **m** and ṣ/ḍ + **r**. Write the combinations (with ṣ; those with ḍ are identical in outline):

ṣ + m: .... صم صم صمي حمم   ṣ + r: .... صر صمر

In pronunciation, these letters 'darken' any adjacent **a** or **ā** just as را rā does (paragraph 1 above). In the list below, dark **a** and **ā** are identified with a dot. *Read and write:*

.... الصّوت الصّوت	aṣ-ṣowt	.... صوت صموت	ṣowt *voice*
.... باص باص	bāṣ *bus*	.... وصول وصول	wuṣūl *arrival*
.... ضرورة ضرورة	ḍarūra *necessity*	.... مصر مصر	miṣr Egypt
.... إضراب إضراب	iḍrāb *strike*	.... مريض مريض	marīḍ *sick* (m.)

Relatives

4   You will have noticed a connection between such words as لبنان
Lebanon and لبناني *Lebanese*.

The first word of the pair is a *noun*, i.e. a word denoting a person, place,
thing or idea (in this case, a place). The second word is either another
noun or an *adjective*, i.e. a word describing a noun. We call this kind of
word a 'relative'. In English we have many ways of making relatives,
but Arabic uses mostly one device, i.e. adding ي... to the base noun.

There are two simple rules for adding the relative ending ي... :

■ the base noun must be in its indefinite form,
■ the ending can be added only to a consonant, so we must remove
    any final vowel (usually a final ا *álif* or a ة *tā marbúṭa*) from the
    base noun.

Applying the first rule, we can derive the relative ياباني *Japanese* from
اليابان *Japan*, taking care first to remove the article from the base noun,
to make it indefinite.

Applying the second rule, we can make ضرورة *necessity* (see the list
immediately above) into the relative ضروري *ḍarúrī necessary*; and
similarly with countless other nouns ending in a vowel which we remove
before adding the relative ending.

Read and write these nouns, most of which you know, and their
relatives:

الماني ..... ألماني	الألمانيا الألمانيا	الألمانيا *al-'almániya Germany*
ليبي ..... ليبي	ليبيا ليبيا	ليبيا* *líbiya Libya*
لبناني ..... لبناني	لبنان لبنان	
ياباني ..... ياباني	اليابان اليابان	
سوري ..... سوري *súrī*	سوريا سوريا	سوريا *súriya Syria*
إيراني ..... إيراني *Iranian*	إيران ايران	
ضروري ..... ضروري	ضرورة ضروره	

أساس ....اساس........ أساسي ....اسـاسـي........ *basic*

رئيس ....رئيـس........ رئيسي ....رئيـسـي........ *main, principal*

دراسة ....د راسه........ دراسي ....د راسي........ *academic*

مصر ....مصر........ مصري ....مصري........ *Egyptian*

ابتداء ....ابتـداء........ ابتدائي ....ابتَدائي........ *primary, initial*

These relatives are in their masculine form, and indefinite. We know from earlier in this book that we can make such words definite (الياباني), or feminine (يابانية), or definite feminine (اليابانية).

* ليبيا is probably the only word of more than one letter in the Arabic language that reads the same backwards as forwards. Try it.

Exercise 2 Make the masculine relative from each of these nouns. Translate your answers:

(a) أساس   (b) مصر   (c) إدارة   (d) ابتداء   (e) وزارة

Exercise 3 Make these relatives definite feminine:

(a) مصري   (b) سوري   (c) إيراني   (d) إسرائيلي*

* isrā´īlī in the masculine. Guess its meaning.

Exercise 4 Transcribe these words, marking with a dot the dark **a**'s and **ā**'s. Why are they dark?

(a) ضرورة   (b) مريض   (c) دراسة   (d) الباص   (e) ملابس

The answers to these exercises are immediately below.

Answers to Exercises

Exercise 1 (a) **al-mudír** *Director*   (b) **ar-ra´īs** *Chairman*
(c) **al-mumáththil** *Representative* (d) **al-´ustádh** *Professor*

Exercise 2 (a) أساسي *basic*   (b) مصري *Egyptian*
(c) إداري *administrative*   (d) ابتدائي *primary, initial*
(e) وزاري *ministerial*

Exercise 3 (a) الإسرائيلية (d) الإيرانية (c) السورية (b) المصرية

Exercise 4 (a) ḍarū́ra, two a's next to r, one next to ḍ (b) marī́ḍ, a next to r (c) dirā́sa, first a next to r (d) al-bāṣ, ā next to ṣ (e) none

Tests

1 Write, paying attention to special connections:

(c) تمام   (b) اهتمام   (a) مصرية

(e) ألماني   (d) ضروري

2 Read aloud your handwritten answers to Test 1.

3 Read aloud:

(c) للسورية   (b) مريض   (a) الإيرانية

(e) بالألمانيا   (d) ابتدائي

4 Give the base word from which the relative is derived. Translate the base word and the relative:

(c) إداري   (b) دراسي   (a) أساسي

(e) الإسرائيلية   (d) للّيبية

5 Pronounce your answers to Test 4. For example, (a) is asā́s.

6 Fill in the missing letter in each word:

(c) مد...ر   (b) إد...رة   (a) الـ..صرية

(e) مريـ..ة   (d) الشـ...ء

Review

In this unit we studied six more letters, including the last four disjoined ones and a pair with 'dark' sounds. You also learned how to derive 'relatives'. This is a big step forward, as there are hundreds of such derived words. You can say that you have added about 10% to your vocabulary at one stroke.

Keep writing. Perhaps your main objective in following this book is to learn how to read; but it is writing which will fix things in your memory.

We have done most of the alphabetical section of this book. There are ten letters to go, all of them in groups or pairs like most of the others; and three more 'curiosities'.

You will have noticed that, because some letters have alternative forms or special connections, you have to think ahead as you write. That gets easier when you begin to see the whole word in your mind; and that comes with practice.

5

In this unit you will learn

■ seven more letters, with their pronunciation,

■ when and how to join these letters,

■ words which you can read and write using the seven letters,

■ more about *stress*.

Letters
1

A family of joined letters, each with a short and full form used exactly like those of ب . The only difference between these three is the dot.

ج jīm sounds like *j* in English *jam* in most Arab countries. In Egypt it sounds like hard *g* in English *go*. We use the sound *j* in this book.

ح ḥā is a heavy *h*; it is the sound made when we breathe on glass to clean it. To an Arab it sounds quite distinct from ه hā, which we learned in Unit 3. Try to make the distinction yourself.

خ kh̲ā represents the sound of *ch* in Scottish *loch* or Welsh *bach*.

The short forms are shallow, resting on the line of writing. The full forms are deep, with a *reverse* half-swoop ﻊ , the head still resting on the line.

Read and write a line of each letter, starting at its top left-hand corner:

An **a** or **ā** next to خ is often (not always) pronounced dark. Imitate what you hear. Don't be confused by the transcription of ح **ḥā**; it is *not* a dark letter. We transcribe it in this manner merely to distinguish it from ه **hā**.

Read and write a few new words:

جنوبي *southern* **janūbī**   جنوب *south* **janū́b**

دخول *entry** **dukhū́l**   خروج *exit** **khurū́j**

* the *action*. The *place* is **mák̲h̲raj** or **mádk̲h̲al**, see below.

When one of these letters is joined to a previous joined letter in print, the connection is often at the right-hand corner of the ج etc.; in handwriting we make the connection at the beginning of the outline, i.e. the left-hand corner. Compare print with handwriting below (for ج only; the others go the same way); practise the handwritten forms:

	handwriting		*print*	
tooth + **j**		بج	سج\بج	
teeth + **j**		سج	سج	
l + **j**		لج	لج\الج	
m + **j**		مج	مج	
s + **j**		سج	سج	

(*and so on, with other preceding joined letters*)

Read and write:

لجنة **lájna** *committee*   احتجاج **iḥtijáj** *objection*

أجنبي **ájnabī** *foreign*   إنتاج **intáj** *production*

مدخل **mádk̲h̲al** *entrance*   مخرج **mák̲h̲raj** *exit*

انتخاب **intik̲h̲áb** *election*   أخبار **ak̲h̲bár** *news*

خاصّ **k̲h̲áṣṣ** *private, special, particular*

2

ط	ṭā
ظ	ẓā

The letters called **ṭā** and **ẓā** are joined letters, yet they have only one form each. It is tall, and always rests on the line. Despite the similarity with ص (Unit 4, paragraph 3), the loop of these letters has no tooth-like projection after it, as does ص. Write a line of these letters, first the loop, then the upright:

ط .... ظ .... ط .... ظ .... ط .... ظ ....

ط .... ظ .... ط .... ظ .... ط .... ظ ....

These are sun letters with dark sounds. Just as ص is the dark equivalent (tongue low, with cavity) of س, so ط is the dark equivalent of ت, and ظ is the dark equivalent of ز. We transcribe ط with **ṭ**, and ظ with **ẓ**. As you might guess, any neighbouring a or ā is darkened. In the list given below, we dot these two vowels for clarity. ***Read and write:***

مطار ..... مطار **maṭā́r** *airport*   طائرة .... طائره ..... **ṭā́'ira** *aeroplane*

وطني .... وطني .... **wáṭanī** *national*   وطن ... وطن ... **wáṭan** *nation*

خطّ ..... خطّا ..... **khaṭṭ** *line*   شرطة .... شرطه ... **shúrṭa** *police*

إيطاليا .... إيطاليا **īṭā́liya** *Italy*   بريطانيا .. بريطانيا **bariṭā́niya** *Britain*

خطر .... خطر ..... **kháṭar** *danger*, **kháṭir** *dangerous*

تنظيم .... تنظيم ..... **tanẓī́m** *organisation* (the activity)

منظمة .... منظمه ..... **munáẓẓama** *organisation* (the body)

Exercise 1 Read the following signs:

Exercise 2 Fill in the missing letter:

(a) إِ...تاج   (b) و...ني   (c) انتـ...اب   (d) ابتـ...ائي   (e) منـ...مة

Exercise 3 List at least twelve nouns beginning with a sun letter, and at least twelve nouns beginning with another (i.e. a 'moon') letter. Make them all definite with the article. Read your answers aloud, and translate them.

Exercise 4 Write, in the masculine singular, all the words you can remember denoting a nationality. Now write all the words you can remember denoting a profession or function. Read everything aloud and translate.

The answers to Exercises 1 and 2 follow paragraph 4.

3

ع ـع ـعـ عـ	9ayn
غ ـغ ـغـ غـ	ghayn

Here comes probably the most difficult sound in the Arabic language. It is the sound of the letter **9ayn**, which we transcribe with **9**, since no letter in our alphabet comes anywhere near its sound. Say to yourself the name *Maggie*. Keep repeating it, but as you do so, try to stop making contact in your throat for the *-gg-* in the middle, i.e. let the middle consonant become more and more vague until it feels no more than a gulp. You are probably saying something like معي **má9ī** *with me*. Now do it again, but get to the target sound faster. Say it again and again until you can hit it first time, without Maggie's help. The correct sound is a little like the name *Marie* as pronounced in French, but without the contact of the French *r*.

The sound of the other letter, which we transcribe as **gh**, is the 'hard' equivalent of **kh**, for which see paragraph 1 above. It sounds somewhat like the French *r* of *Marie*, but shorter.

ع and غ are joined letters. The two short forms rest on the line, and the two full forms have a reverse half-swoop like ح . The different forms are used as follows:

- ﻌ and ﻐ are written at the beginning of a word, or in the middle of a word after a *disjoined* letter,
- ـﻌ and ـﻐ are written in the middle of a word after a *joined* letter,
- ـﻊ and ـﻎ are written at the end of a word after a *joined* letter,
- ﻉ and ﻍ are written at the end of a word after a *disjoined* letter, or when standing alone.

Or we can put it far more simply: the 'solid' forms stand after a joined letter, and the 'open' forms stand everywhere else.

Write several of each:

Read and write:

سعر سعر	si9r *price*	عامّ عامّ	9ámm *general, public*
مطعم مطعم	mát9am *restaurant*	صناعة صناعة	şiná9a *industry*
معلم معلّم	mu9állim *teacher*	أسبوع اسبوع	usbú9 *week*
شارع شارع	shári9 *street*	اجتماع اجتماع	ijtimá9 *meeting*
غربي غربي	ghárbī *western*	غرب غرب	gharb *west*
مشغول مشغول	mashghúl *busy*	مبلغ مبلغ	máblagh *sum*

Stress

4 So far we have marked the stress (see Unit 1, paragraph 4) with an accent. But Arabic stress is almost entirely regular, and we can learn and apply simple rules:

■ the stress falls on the last so-called 'heavy' syllable if there is one. A 'heavy' syllable is one with either

- a long vowel (ā, ī, ū) or a vowel-combination (**ay, ou, ow**) followed by a consonant (**b, j, d** etc.): **bināyát, marī́ḍ, usbū́9, bintáyn**,

- or a short vowel (**a, i, u**) followed by two consonants* or a doubled consonant: **máblagh, mumáththil**,

  * Remember that consonants transcribed with underlining (**th, gh** etc.) are single consonants in Arabic.

■ if there is no heavy syllable, the first syllable is stressed: **ána**.

The following elements are never stressed, and are not counted when placing the stress:

■ the article **al-, at-** (etc.),

■ any vowel (long or short) or vowel-combination ending a word, i.e. with no following consonant. Note that **hámza**, although not an alphabetical letter, counts as a consonant, so that a word like **ibtidá'** does not end in a vowel; its final syllable counts as heavy, and is herefore stressed. The relative of this word has the same stress (**ibtidá'ī**).

Now that we have the rules, we no longer need to mark the stress in the transcription.

Exercise 5 Read the signs:

 (d) (c) (b) (a)

Exercise 6 Mark the stress with an accent on these transcribed words or word-forms which we have not yet studied:

(a) **mashghūlīn**   (b) **maḥaṭṭa**   (c) **intikhābāt**   (d) **tarbiya**

Exercise 7 Complete the word with the right form of ع or غ :

(a) ...اجتما (b) مشـ...ـول (c) مـ...ـلمة (d) مبلـ... (e) ...امّ

Exercise 8 Write in Arabic (putting any relatives or other adjectives in the m. form), and pronounce your answers, taking care with the stress:

(a) *the meeting* (b) *daily* (c) *monthly* (d) *arrival* (e) *south*
(f) *the week* (g) *electoral* (h) *the school* (j) *Italian* (k) *administrative*

Exercise 9 Reading. Covering everything but the printed Arabic, read again, column by column, the 'Read and write' paragraphs of this unit.

The answers to Exercises 5 to 8 are immediately below.

Answers to Exercises

Exercise 1 (a) íbil *CAMELS** (b) bāṣ *BUS* (c) khátar *DANGER*

Exercise 2 (a) إنتاج (b) وطني (c) انتـخاب (d) ابتـدائي (e) منظّمة

Exercise 5 (a) shurṭa (b) makhraj (c) madkhal (d) shimāl

Exercise 6 (a) mashghūlín (b) maḥáṭṭa (c) intikhābāt (d) tárbiya

Exercise 7 (a) اجتماع (b) مشغول (c) معلمة (d) مبلغ (e) عامّ

Exercise 8 (a) الاجتماع al-ijtimā9 (b) يومي yóumī
(c) شهري sháhrī (d) وصول wuṣūl (e) جنوب janūb
(f) الأسبوع al-'usbū9 (g) انتخابي intikhắbī (h) المدرسة al-mádrasa
(j) إيطالي īṭắlī (k) إداري idárī

---

* This picturesque desert-road warning should be taken seriously, especially if visibility is poor. In a collision, most animals fall under the car. But the camel is hit below his knees, with possibly appalling consequences for both man and beast. The stricken and struggling animal, his already considerable weight increased by the impact, comes crashing through the car roof.

The camel deserves respect. He is silent and can be swift. And the desert is his.

Tests

1   Read aloud and translate these words:

(c) السِّعر   (b) مسؤولة   (a) الشَّيْء

(e) الانتخاب   (d) مدخَل

2   Arrange these in the order of their size, biggest first:

(c) الأسبوع   (b) السَّنة   (a) اليوم

(d) الشهر

3   Make a relative, in the indefinite masculine form, from each noun.
    Give its meaning:

(c) الأسبوع   (b) ابتداء   (a) الصِّناعة

(d) ايطاليا   (e) بريطانيا

4   Write:
    (a) **at-ta'sīs**   (b) **an-nihā'ī**   (c) **mas'ūla**
    (d) **al-makhraj**   (e) **ad-dukhūl**

Review

In this unit we covered seven more joined letters, two of them sun
letters with dark sounds; and many useful new words. You also
learned how to stress correctly any word in the language.

The next unit gives us the remaining three letters and three
'curiosities', rounding off the alphabetical part of this book.

6

In this unit you will learn

■ the remaining three letters, and three special spellings, with their pronunciation,

■ the full alphabet in its proper order,

■ how Arabic transcribes foreign words.

Letters

1

ف ـفـ ف	fā
ق ـقـ ق	qāf

The joined letter ف ـفـ ف **fā** represents *f* as in English *fee*. The joined letter ق ـقـ ق **qāf**, which we can transcribe as **q**, is pronounced like *k* in English, but as far back in the throat as possible. Say *coo* several times, taking the contact back as far as you can. The result is **q**. The letter ق does *not* represent an English *q* in sound.

The short and full forms are used in the manner known to you. The full form of **fā** is shallow like the ب group, while the full form of **qāf** is deep with a swoop, like ن . Both **fā** and **qāf** are dotted above the ring, in both short and full forms. Write several:

In Tunisia, Algeria and Morocco you may find ب ـبـ ب for **fā** and ف ـفـ ف for **qāf**; in Morocco you can see signs indicating the city of باس **fās** *Fez*. In this book we use the much commoner forms of the letters, shown in the box.

Since ق has a dark sound, any neighbouring **a** or **ā** is darkened. The dark vowels are dotted in the examples given below. Read and write:

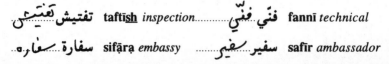

تفتيش **taftīsh** *inspection* .... فنّي **fannī** *technical*

سفارة **sifāra** *embassy* .... سفير **safīr** *ambassador*

رقم ....رَقَم.... **rạqm** *number*   مفتوح ....مفتوح.... **maftūḥ** *open*

شرق ....شرق.... **shạrq** *east*   قف قف ....قف.... **qif** *STOP* (on road signs)

سوق ....سوق.... **sūq** *market*   تقرير....تقرير.... **tạqrīr** *report, decision*

العراق ....العراق.... **al-9irạq** *Iraq*   القاهرة ....القاهره.... **al-qạhira** *Cairo*

2

ك ك **kāf**

The letter ك ك **kāf** represents the sound *k* as in English *book*. It is a tall joined letter, with short and full forms used in the manner known to you. The forms you see here are printed forms; in handwriting the short form is upright, while in the full form the small embellishment ˙ becomes a hook inside the curve (like the dot of ن , see Unit 1). The differences are shown below:

handwriting: ....ك ....ك....   *print and type:* ك ك

Write several handwritten forms:

............ك ....ك ....ك ....ك ....ك ....ك ....ك

............ك ....ك ....ك ....ك ....ك ....ك ....ك

The 'headstroke' of the short form, and the hook of the long form, serve to make sure that this letter does not get confused with ل ل . You will also meet the printed isolated form ك , not used in handwriting. Read and write:

شركة ....شركة.... **shạrika** *company*   كبير ....كبير.... **kabīr** *big*

ممكن ....ممكن.... **mumkin** *possible*   مكتب ....مكتب.... **maktab** *office*

بنك ....بنك.... **bank** *bank*

There are special handwritten forms for the combinations **kāf-alif**, **kāf-lām** and **kāf-lām-alif**. Copy the handwritten forms from this table:

handwriting	*print*
كا كا ﻩﺗ	كا
كل كل كل ﻩﺗ	كل كل\كل
كلا كلا ﻩﺗ	كلا

Now *read and write:*

إمكانية امكانيه   **imkānīya** *possibility*   كاتب كاتب   **kātib** *writer*

مشكلة مشكله   **mushkila** *problem*   كل كلّ   **kull** *every, all*

تكليف تكليف   **taklīf** *cost*   كلام كلام   **kalām** *speech, speaking*

Exercise 1 Write these new words:

(a) **akthar** *more*   (b) **shakl** *form*   (c) **kammīya** *quantity*

(d) **miftāḥ** *key*   (e) **iqtirāḥ** *proposal*

Exercise 2 Given the word مكتوب **maktūb** *written* as a model, you can easily read words with the same pattern such as مربوط **marbūṭ** *connected*, معلوم **ma9lūm** *known*, منشور **manshūr** *published*. Now read these new words, following the model given:

(a) كاتب **kātib** *writer*. Read عامل *worker*, سائق *driver*, ساكن *resident*

(b) كبير **kabīr** *big*. Read كثير *much*, صغير *small*, فقير *poor*, قليل *little, few*, قريب *near*

(c) استقبال **istiqbāl** *reception*. Read استكشاف *exploration*, استثمار *investment*, استعمال *use*, استنكار *rejection*, استقلال *independence*

(d) تفتيش **taftīsh** *inspection*. Read تقسيم *partition*, تحسين *repair*, تعليم *tuition*

(e) مكتب **maktab** *office*. Read مطبخ *kitchen*, متحف *museum*, مشغل *workshop*, مصنع *factory*, ملعب *playground, playing-field*

(f) ممثّل **mumaththil** *representative*. Read مفتّش *inspector*, مقرّر *reporter*, مدرّس *instructor*, محرّك *engine*

The answers to these exercises follow paragraph 6 below.

3

 أً اً tanwīn

Now that you have learned the alphabet, here are three curiosities for you. The first two, shown in the box above, are called **tanwīn***, which we can translate as '*en-ing*' or 'providing with *n*'. Here they are in action:

فوراً **fouran** *immediately*   عادةً **9ādatan** *usually*

The one with alif, اً, is always pronounced **-an** (short a, despite the alif), while the one with tā marbūṭa, ةً , is pronounced **-atan**. The dots of ة are always written in handwriting for this form. When **tanwīn** is added to the ending -ī the combination becomes ـيةً...\ ـياً... **-īyan/-īyatan**. We write **tanwīn** only at the end of a word, and it is useful because it marks countless *adverbs*, i.e. words describing verbs or adjectives. In some print, and, alas, in much handwriting, the ً... mark is omitted, leaving us with اً... and ةً... which is not very helpful. In this book the ً... is always shown, and you are advised always to write it. The *n* sound is *not* written with ن in this special form.

* There are in fact three **tanwīns**, one for each of the vowels **a, i** and **u**; but you will hardly ever see the last two, and they need not concern us. The full name of the useful one shown here is **alif tanwīn**. We can call it simply **tanwīn**.

Read and write:

رسمياً،رسمياً **rasmīyan** *officially*......... كثيراً كثيراً **kathīran** *greatly*

قليلاً قليلٌ **qalīlan** *a little*......... مثلاً مثلاً **mathalan** *for example*

خاصةً خاصةً **khāssatan** *specially*

4

ى alif maqṣūra

This one is our third curiosity. In some words you will see a final yā, without the dots, which is not pronounced -ī at all, but which sounds -a, just like final ‍ا alif. This form is called **alif maqṣūra**. It occurs in only a few words. Pronounce it **-a**. This 'curiosity' can be confusing.

The situation is not helped by the fact that ي proper (the one that is pronounced **-ī**), when standing alone, is often printed and handwritten without its dots: you will, for example, see مصرى for مصري **miṣrī**.

Two things are worth noting, and they offer some help:

■ when you see ى it is much more likely to be **yā** (sounded **-ī**) which is much more common than **alif maqṣūra** (sounded **-a**),

■ **alif maqṣūra** occurs only at the end of a word, nowhere else.

Throughout this book we write ي for isolated **yā** and ى only for **alif maqṣūra**. You are recommended to do the same, to make your handwriting clear.

Read and write:

على..عل............ 9ala *on*   إلى..الى............ ila *to*

مستشفى..مــتـشــفى mustashfa *hospital*

Exercise 3 Which way, right or left, to (a) *school*, (b) *hospital*, (c) *airport*, (d) *market*? Read the words aloud:

The answers to this exercise follow paragraph 6 below.

Alphabet

5   Here is the whole alphabet, in its Arabic order. Read from the middle outwards, as you always should when you have parallel Arabic and English columns:

←   →

ا   alif

ب ت ث   bā tā <u>th</u>ā

ج ح خ   jīm ḥā <u>kh</u>ā

د ذ	dāl dhāl
ر ز	rā zayy
س ش	sīn shīn
ص ض	ṣād ḍād
ط ظ	ṭā ẓā
ع غ	9ayn ghayn
ف ق ك	fā qāf kāf
ل م ن	lām mīm nūn
ه و ي	hā wow yā

Special letters, and signs not found in the alphabet, are usually listed as follows:

آ, أ and إ	with ا
ة	with ه
ؤ	with ا or و
ئ\ء	with ا or ي
ى	with ي
ٌ...	is disregarded

Using this order, you can look up a proper name or a department etc. in a list or directory such as a telephone book or street index; also in the vocabulary in this book. You can also use a dictionary, provided you use one of the newer ones which list alphabetically by *words*: examples are Steingass' Arabic-English Dictionary published by Khayat in Beirut, or a later edition of 'Al-Mawrid', Arabic-English, published by Dar al-Ilm li-l-Malayin, also of Beirut.

If you understand German, you can use Langenscheidt's Arabic-German/German-Arabic dictionary, either the pocket or the desk edition. This is also arranged alphabetically by words, with transcription.

Avoid older Arabic-English dictionaries: they may be good, but they list by *roots*, and you have to know Arabic grammar well to find your word.

The vocabularies in this book are arranged alphabetically by words.

Exercise 4 Put these customer files in their right alphabetical order:

　(f)　　　　(e)　　　　(d)　　　　(c)　　　　(b)　　　　(a)

Match the transcriptions to the names: **mūsa, bilāl, ḥasanayn, <u>sh</u>amsī, sulaymān, <u>kh</u>ūrī**.

Now imagine opening three fresh files in the names of (g) **zaydān**, (h) **abūbakr** and (j) **nūrī**. Write these names and put them in alphabetical order with the others.

The answers to this exercise follow paragraph 6 below.

Arabic Transcription

6　　There is no standard Arabic transcription for foreign words. But the following principles seem generally to be followed.

Little distinction is made between foreign long and short vowels: ‏ا‎ is used for long and short *a*, ‏و‎ for long and short *u* and *o*, and ‏ي‎ for long and short *e* and *i*.

v is usually transcribed either with ‏ف‎ or the artificial letter ‏ڤ‎; *p* either with ‏ب‎ or the Persian/Urdu letter ‏پ‎; *g* with ‏ك‎ or ‏ج‎, and *ch* with the Persian/Urdu letter ‏چ‎:

‏فيينا\ڤيينا‎ **viyēnā** *Vienna*　　　　　‏باريس‎ **pārīs** *Paris*

‏جنيف‎ **jinēv** (Fr. *Genève*) *Geneva*　　‏روما‎ **rōma** *Rome*

‏تلفون\تليفون‎ **tilifōn/tilīfōn** *telephone*　‏كمبيوتر‎ **kampyūtir** *computer*

‏أوتوبيس‎ **otobīs** (Fr. *autobus*) *bus*　　‏أوتيل‎ **ōtēl** (Fr. *hôtel*) *hotel*

As you know, in Egypt ‏ج‎ is pronounced like hard English *g* (see Unit 5), so you often see ‏چ‎ for **j** in foreign names in Egypt: ‏جاكارتا‎ Jakarta.

Initial *s* followed by a consonant other than *w* is transcribed as ‏أس...‎:

‏اسكتلندا‎ **iskotlanda** *Scotland*, but: ‏سويسرا‎ **swisira** *Switzerland*.

When reading a commercial sign, remember that it is possibly not Arabic at all. Try reading it aloud, especially if it has no recognisable Arabic shape. I used to enjoy watching people puzzle over a shop sign in the Arabian Gulf which read فيش أند چيپس; it sometimes took them a minute to realise that they could go inside and order the local equivalent of cod-and-fries, and even wash it down with a cool فانتا, a سيڤن آپ or a بيبسي كولا.

Answers to Exercises

Exercise 1 (a) اقتراح (e)   مفتاح (d)   كمّية (c) شكل (b) أكثر

Exercise 2 (a) 9āmil, sā'iq, sākin

(b) kathīr, ṣaghīr, faqīr, qarīb, qalīl

(c) istik<u>sh</u>āf, isti<u>th</u>mār, isti9māl, istinkār, istiqlāl

(d) taqsīm, taḥsīn, ta9līm

(e) maṭba<u>kh</u>, matḥaf, ma<u>sh</u>gh<u></u>al, maṣna9, mal9ab

(f) mufatti<u>sh</u>, muqarrir, mudarris, muḥarrik

Exercise 3 (a) مدرسة madrasa, left; (b) مستشفى musta<u>sh</u>fa, right; (c) مطار maṭār, right; (d) سوق sūq, left.

Exercise 4 (f) bilāl (b) ḥasanayn (d) <u>kh</u>ūrī (e) sulaymān (c) shamsī (a) mūsa.

(g) زيدان goes before (e), (h) أبويكر goes first, and (j) نوري goes last.

Tests

1 Read aloud and translate:

(a) صناعة   (b) مطار   (c) مسؤول

(d) وزارة   (e) إدارة   (f) أخبار

(g) احتجاج   (h) شركة   (j) أو

(k) سوق   (m) مثلاً   (n) مستشفى

2 Rewrite the word, filling in the missing letter. Read your answer aloud.

(a) مــ...لم   (b) مــ...تب   (c) فور...

(d) تــ...سيس   (e) ابتــ..ائي

3 You certainly know these international brand names. Read them aloud:

(a) كوداك   (b) آي بي إم   (c) مـوبيل

(d) ميشلين   (e) بيجو*

*(e) difficult. Every single letter in this French name is at best an approximation.

Review

We have now completed the alphabet and the various signs commonly used in writing.

If you are in an Arab country while working through this book, you should already be able to make sense of some of the words shown on signs and notices around you.

7

In this unit you will learn

■ how to make words *dual* (two of a kind) and *plural* (more than two of a kind),

■ how to read and write figures.

Word Forms

1   Dual

You will occasionally see the ending ...ين -ayn or ...أن -ān added to a word. This is the so-called 'dual' ending, and it means 'two'. English uses a number for 'two'; Arabic uses an ending.

A final ة on the original word changes to ت , and a final ى (**alif maqṣura**, see Unit 6 paragraph 4) changes to ي , before the dual ending is added.

The relative ending ي together with the dual ending becomes ...يين -īyayn or ...يان -īyān. *Read and write:*

مديران مديران	mudirān	مديرين مديرين	mudirayn
مكتبان مكتبان	maktabān	مكتبين مكتبين	maktabayn
وزارتان وزارتان	wizāratān	وزارتين وزارتين	wizāratayn
شركتان شركتان	sharikatān	شركتين شركتين	sharikatayn
لبنانيان\لبنانيين لبنانيان لبنانيان	lubnānīyayn/lubnānīyān		
مستشفيين مستشفيين	mustashfayayn		
مستشفيان مستشفيان	mustashfayān		

two directors, two offices, two ministries, two companies, two Lebanese (m.)*, two hospitals*

The two endings are not interchangeable. You will find the ...ين -ayn series (the first one shown) much more common, and you should use it for preference when in doubt. We will have some guidelines later.

The dual ending is always *stressed*: -áyn/-ā́n.

2   Plural endings

Remember that whereas for English 'plural' means 'more than one', for Arabic it means 'more than *two*'.

There are two endings we can add to words to make them plural (pl.).

The commonest plural ending you will meet is ...ات . This is known as the *feminine* plural ending.

This is added to almost all nouns ending in ة , whatever their meaning (the ة is dropped before the plural ending is added), and to many nouns denoting things, places or ideas, whatever their ending.

It is also added to the very few nouns ending in ى , which of course changes to ي before the plural ending is added. ***Read and write:***

اتنخابات انتخابات	intikhābāt	انتخاب انتخاب	intikhāb
شركات شركات	sharikāt	شركة شركة	sharika
معلمات معلمات	mu9allimāt	معلمة معلمة	mu9allima
	مستشفى مستشفى		mustashfa
	مستشفيات مستشفيات		mustashfayāt

election(s), company/-ies, teacher(s) (f.), hospital(s)

The second commonest plural ending is ...ين -īn, with its rarer variant ...ون -ūn.

This ending is added only to a few words denoting male persons. It is known as the *masculine* plural ending.

The relative ending ي together with this plural ending becomes ...يين -īyīn (less commonly, ...يون -īyūn). ***Read and write:***

معلمون معلمون	mu9allimūn	معلمين معلمين	mu9allimīn
ممثلون ممثلون	mumaththilūn	ممثلين ممثلين	mumaththilīn
مفتشون مفتشون	mufattishūn	مفتشين مفتشين	mufattishīn
إيطاليون إيطاليون	īṭālīyūn	إيطاليين إيطاليين	īṭālīyīn

teacher(s), representative(s), inspector(s), Italian(s) - all masculine.

As with the dual, so the two masculine plural endings are not interchangeable. The ين... -īn series is much more common, and you should use it for preference when in doubt. We will have some guidelines later.

The masculine plural ending is always *stressed*: -**īn**/-**ūn**.

3   Irregular plurals

Very many words make their plurals not by adding an ending, but by changing their internal shape. We have this phenomenon with a few English words; consider the singular 'man' with its plural 'men', or 'mouse' and 'mice'. Irregular plural patterns are very common in Arabic. Many such patterns exist, and, unfortunately for us, we can give no rules. An irregular plural form has to be learned together with its singular.

A few important patterns are listed below, with a model word for each pattern.

It looks a formidable list. *Don't* try to learn it: simply take note that such patterns exist, and use the list for reference. The important thing is that when you meet an unfamiliar irregular plural, you check whether you know a singular noun with the same consonants in the same order. If you do, there is a good chance that you have broken the code and identified the meaning. Using a foreign language often involves astute detective work and intelligent guessing.

Read and write the examples:

	irregular plural		*singular*

(a) model a**kh**bār:

أخبار اخبار	akhbār	خبر خبر	**kh**abar	} news
انباء أنباء	anbā'	نبأ نبأ	naba'	item
اسعار أسعار	as9ār	سعر سعر	si9r *price*
اخطار أخطار	akhṭār	خطر خطر	**kh**aṭar *danger*
اشياء أشياء	ashyā'	شيء شيء	**sh**ay' *thing*
افلام أفلام	aflām	فلم فلم	film *film*

(b) model **buyūt**:

بيوت بيوت	**buyūt**	بيت	**bayt** *house*
خطوط خطوط	**khuṭūṭ**	خطّ	**khaṭṭ** *line*
بنوك بنوك	**bunūk**	بنك	**bank** *bank*
هنود هنود	**hunūd**	هندي	**hindī** *Indian*

(c) model **madāris**:

مدارس مدارس	**madāris**	مدرسة مدرسة	**madrasa** *school*
مشاكل مشاكل	**mashākil**	مشكلة مشكلة	**mushkila** *problem*
مكاتب مكاتب	**makātib**	مكتب مكتب	**maktab** *office*
مخارج مخارج	**makhārij**	مخرج مخرج	**makhraj** *exit*
مداخل مداخل	**madākhil**	مدخل مدخل	**madkhal** *entrance*

(d) model **asābī9**:

أسابيع أسابيع	**asābī9**	أسبوع أسبوع	**usbū9** *week*
مفاتيح مفاتيح	**mafātiḥ**	مفتاح مفتاح	**miftāḥ** *key*

(e) model **mudarā'**:

مدراء مدراء	**mudarā'**	مدير مدير	**mudīr** *director*
وزراء وزراء	**wuzarā'**	وزير وزير	**wazīr** *minister*

(f) model **9arab**:

عرب عرب	**9arab**	عربي عربي	**9arabī** *Arab, Arabic, Arabian*
إنجليز إنجليز	**ingilīz**	إنجليزي إنجليزي	**ingilīzī** *English, British*
يهود يهود	**yahūd**	يهودي يهودي	**yahūdī** *Jew(ish)*

and many other patterns.

Some words have alternative plurals, one with an ending, one irregular; or even two irregular forms. Sometimes the alternatives have different meanings. An example is تقرير taqrīr *report, decision*, plurals تقارير taqārīr *reports*, تقريرات taqrīrāt *decisions*.

Another important word with alternative plural forms is أميركي amayrkī *American*, plurals أميركيين\...يون amayrkīyīn/-īyūn or أميركان amayrkān.

Three final things to note about plural and dual forms:

- All the duals and plurals can be made definite with the article, as usual: المدراء, المعلمين, الشركات, المديرين.
- When a noun has a regular plural, we add the masculine ending (ين\...ون...) to a noun denoting a male person, or to show mixed company, male and female; we add the feminine regular ending (ات...) to a noun denoting a female person, *and* to a noun denoting anything other than a person.
- The -ayn ending and the -īn ending are both written ين... . There can be confusion. There is a means of marking the difference, but you never see it in use. In general, read -īn if in doubt.

In the rest of this book, irregular plurals of new words will be given with the singular, so: بيت بيوت bayt buyūt. Where no plural is marked, it is regular, i.e. is formed with an ending, as shown above.

Exercise 1 Here are some plurals. Give the singular form of the word:

(a) مدراء (b) سيّارات (c) تلفونات (d) مفتّشين (e) خطوط

Exercise 2 Put the words together in singular/plural pairs:

بنايات، مدير، مفتّش، بناية، وزراء، وزارات، شركات، بيوت مدراء، مفتّشين، وزير، معلمة، وزارة، شركة، معلّمات، بيت.

Exercise 3 Make the relative form, in the feminine:

(a) أميركا* (b) وطن (c) باكستان* (d) إسرائيل* (e) العراق

* New foreign words. Easy, if you say them aloud.

Exercise 4 (a), (b) and (c) below are signs and notices which we have read before. Can you fill in the missing captions? Having done that, read, pronounce and translate the new sign, (d):

Exercise 5 Look back at Unit 6, Exercise 2. Read these new words, following the model given:

(a) كتّاب **kuttāb** *writers*. Read زوّار *visitors*, عمّال *workmen*, نوّاب *deputies*.

(b) مكتوب **maktūb** *written*. Read ممنوع *prohibited*, مطبوع *printed*, معروف *known*, مكتوم *confidential*.

(c) مدرسة **madrasa** *school*. Read مكتب *library/bookshop*, محكمة *law-court*.

(d) سياحة **siyāḥa** *tourism*. Read نجارة *carpentry*, سباكة *plumbing*, خياطة *sewing*.

The answers to these exercises follow paragraph 4 below.

Figures

4 Figures are written as follows. Most important: they are written from *left to right*, like European figures. Write the handwritten forms shown below the printed forms:
→→

1	١	١	١	2	٢	٢	٢
	١	١	١		٢	٢	٢
3	٣	٣	٣	4	٤	٤	٤
	١٢٣	١٢٣	١٢٣		٤	٤	٤
5	٥	٥	٥	6	٦	٦	٦
	٥	٥	٥		٦	٦	٦

7	٧	٧	٧	8	٨	٨	٨
	٧	٧	٧		٨	٨	٨
9	٩	٩	٩	0	٠	٠	٠
	٩	٩	٩		٠	٠	٠

Be careful with handwritten figures ٢ (٢) and ٣ or ٣ (٣). Many people write ٣ for extra clarity. It is not wrong to copy the printed forms in handwriting if you prefer; though some Arabs may read your ٢ as a handwritten ٣.

Don't confuse ٥ (5) with ٠ (0).

When figures occur with letters or symbols, they should be read like this: ب ٥٩٨ as *598 B*; ٪٦٤ as *64%*. Reading in both directions needs a little practice.

In Morocco, Algeria, Tunisia and Libya the European figures are used.

There is more about numbers, including how they are pronounced, in Unit 13.

Exercise 6 Write in Arabic figures:

(a) *2487*   (b) *503*   (c) *1999*   (d) *1420*   (e) *2006*

Exercise 7 Write in European figures:

٤٠٥ (e)   ١٠٠٠ (d)   ٢٠٥٧ (c)   ١٦٢ (b)   ٤٣٨٥ (a)

Exercise 8 Copy in Arabic figures and letters these car number-plates in handwriting. Then put them into European figures and letters:

(c)

(b)   (a)

The answers to these exercises are on the next page.

Answers to Exercises

Exercise 1 (a) مدير (b) سيّارة (c) تلفون (d) مفتّش (e) خطّ

Exercise 2

بناية، بنايات؛ مدير، مدراء؛ مفتّش، مفتّشين؛ وزير، وزراء؛
وزارة، وزارات؛ شركة، شركات؛ بيت، بيوت؛ معلمة، معلمات.

Exercise 3 (a) أميركية (b) وطنية (c) باكستانية (d) إسرائيلية
(e) عراقية

Exercise 4 (a) مخرج (b) تمهّل (c) خطر (d) qif *STOP*

Exercise 5 (a) zuwwār, 9ummāl, nuwwāb
(b) mamnū9, maṭbū9, ma9rūf, maktūm
(c) maktaba, maḥkama
(d) nijāra, sibāka, khiyāṭa

Exercise 6 (a) ٢٤٨٧   (b) ٥٠٣   (c) ١٩٩٩   (d) ١٤٢٠
(e) ٢٠٠٦

Exercise 7 (a) *4385*   (b) *162*   (c) *2057*   (d) *1000*   (e) *405*

Exercise 8 (a) س ٤٨٩٢٣ *48923 S*   (b) ٤٨٢٧٦-٤٥ *48376-45*
(c) ٧٩-٦٣٢٧ *79 6327*

Tests

1   Read aloud and translate:

(c) شركة	(b) القاهرة	(a) العراق
(f) إداري	(e) زيارة	(d) ممكن
(j) محكمة	(h) السّوريين	(g) ممثّلين
(n) الانتخابات	(m) مدارس	(k) أجنبي

2   Arrange these iregular plurals into groups, each group with its model
(which is included to help you). Don't worry about the words you
don't know; it is the pattern which counts:

مشاكل، أسابيع، خطوط، ظروف، مطاعم، أرقام، عواصم،
أموال، وزراء، بيوت، مبالغ، مدراء، أخبار، محاكم، أساليب،
وكلاء، أفكار، مدارس، بنوك.

3   Make the masculine plural relative, in the indefinite form (e.g. لبنانيين), from each word:

(a) سوريا   (b) إيران   (c) مصر

(d) العراق   (e) الكويت*

*(e) unfair - we haven't done this proper name. But it is familiar and you can handle it. Just follow the rules.

4   Make these words plural. They all follow the feminine regular pattern:

(a) البناية   (b) السفارة   (c) مستشفى

(d) كمبيوتر   (e) أوتيل   (f) معلمة

(g) المطار   (h) منظمة   (j) شركة

(k) إمكانية   (m) الزيارة   (n) انتخاب

Review

We have learned the dual and the plural, regular and irregular. Don't be discouraged by the variety of irregular plurals; Arabs often have similar difficulty. The commonest patterns become more familiar with practice.

Next we learn some of the word-patterns which characterise Arabic - and which help us to find our way around a language whose words are very different from our own.

8

In this unit you will learn
- three important forms derived from verbs,
- something about other writing styles.

Verbal Forms
1 Participles

Think of English words like 'writer', 'writing', 'written'. The first one names a person *doing an action*; the second describes such a person. The third describes a thing *suffering an action*.

All three are derived from a verb (in this case *to write*), but they are not verbs themselves. They are either *nouns* or *adjectives* (look back to Unit 4, paragraph 4 if you are unsure of these terms).

Arabic has such words too, and they are numerous and useful. We call them **participles**. The ones referring to a *person or thing doing an action* (*writer*, *writing* in English) are called **active participles**. The ones referring to a *person or thing suffering an action* (*written* in English) are called **passive participles**.

Both active and passive varieties can be used either as nouns or as adjectives, as long as the words make sense.

Arabic participles have recognisable patterns, fortunately not too many to learn. Here are the main ones, grouped according to a model, with examples, which you will find useful. Obviously, a verb has both active and passive participles only where both would make sense or be useful. For most verbs, only one of the two is in common use. The columns shown below (active on the left, passive on the right) reflect this fact.

Approach this list in the same way as you did the irregular plural patterns listed in Unit 7. What is familiar will stick in your memory straight away, giving you the pattern. Practice, and inquisitiveness, will help you to apply the pattern more widely.

Read and write (there is, alas, no room to show the handwriting here):

Active Participle ('doing')	Passive Participle ('suffering')

(a) model **kātib** (active), **maktūb** (passive):

كاتب كتّاب **kātib kuttāb**
writer, clerk

مكتوب **maktūb** *written*

سائق **sā'iq** *driver*

عامل عمّال **9āmil 9ummāl** *workman*

لازم **lāzim** *necessary*

حاضر **ḥāḍir** *present, ready*

مفتوح **maftūḥ** *open(ed)*

ممنوع **mamnū9** *prohibited*

مشغول **mashghūl** *busy ('busied')*

معلومات **ma9lumāt**
('things known') information

محفوظ **maḥfūẓ** *reserved*

(b) model **mumaththil** (active), **mumaththal** (passive):

ممثّل **mumaththil** *representative*   ممثّل **mumaththal** *represented*

مفتّش **mufattish** *inspector*

معلّم **mu9allim** *teacher*

مدرّس **mudarris** *instructor*

مقرّر **muqarrir** *reporter*

مقرّر **muqarrar** *decided*

(c) model **musā9id** (active; no common passives):

مساعد **musā9id** *assistant*

مسافر **musāfir** *traveller*

محامي **muḥāmī** *lawyer*

محاسب **muḥāsib** *accountant*

مناسب **munāsib** *appropriate*

(d) model **mursil** (active), **mursal** (passive):

مرسل **mursil** *sender*

مرسل **mursal** *sent*

معطي **mu9ṭī** *donor*

مفيد **mufīd** *useful*

مهمّ **muhimm** *important*

(e) model **muntakhib** (active), **muntakhab** (passive):

منتخب **muntakhib** *elector*	منتخب **muntakhab** *elected*
مشترك **mushtarik** *participant*	مشترك **mushtarak** *joint,*
متّحد **muttahid** *united*	*common*
منتظر **muntazir** *waiting for*	منتظر **muntazar** *awaited*

(f) model **mustakhdim** (active), **mustakhdam** (passive):

مستخدم **mustakhdim** *employer*	مستخدم **mustakhdam** *employed*
مستقبل **mustaqbil** *(radio, TV) receiver*	مستقبل **mustaqbal** *future*
مستعدّ ل **musta9idd li-** *ready for*	

You can see that

■ a few active participles of model (a) have an irregular plural, in the masculine form, almost all other participles (passive of model (a), and active and passive of models (b) to (f)) having regular plurals.

■ in models (b) to (f), the only difference in form between the active and passive forms is in the last vowel: **-i-** for the active, **-a-** for the passive. Unfortunately, everyday Arabic writing does not show this important difference. There is a way of marking it, but this is seldom used outside school textbooks. We have to be guided by the context.

The participle can be made feminine and/or plural, as usual:

معلمة **mu9allima** *teacher* (f.)   سائقين **sā'iqīn** *drivers*

Exercise 1 Read aloud the participles listed after each model:

(a) model كاتب: وارد *arriving,* طالب *student,* كامل *complete,* عارف *knowing*

(c) model مساعد: محافظ *conservative,* مقابل *facing*

(f) model مستخدم: مستعمل *user,* مستأجر *tenant,* مستثمر *investor*

What is the last vowel in all these participles? How do you know?

Exercise 2 Read aloud these passive participles:

مكسور *broken,* مستنكر *rejected,* مسلح *armed,* مقترح *proposed*

The answers to these exercises follow paragraph 4 below.

Verbal Nouns

2   Think of the English word 'inspection'. It comes from a verb ('to inspect') but is itself a noun. It denotes the *activity* of the verb. Arabic has countless nouns of this kind; we call them **verbal nouns**. We know the verbal noun *inspection* in Arabic, from Unit 6: it is تفتيش **taftīsh**.

Verbal nouns are important in Arabic. We meet them constantly in notices etc. The ones corresponding to the group (a) participles (model كاتب\مكتوب) are irregular in form, but groups (b) to (f), corresponding to the participle groups (b) to (f), are regular, following known models in the same way as do the participles.

The following list is *not* intended for learning outright. Treat it mainly as reference material; some of it is familiar already. ***Read and write:***

(a) irregular (several patterns are found; the words are best learned simply as nouns):

كتابه كتابة	كتابة	**kitāba** (the act of) *writing*
وصول وصول	وصول	**wuṣūl** *arrival*
عمل أعمال عمل اعمال		**9amal a9māl** *work*

(b) model **taftīsh**:

تفتيش تفتيش	تفتيش	**taftīsh** *inspection*
تعليم تعليم	تعليم	**ta9līm** *tuition, education*
تنظيم تنظيم	تنظيم	**tanẓīm** (act of) *organisation*
تقرير تقرير	تقرير	**taqrīr** *report, decision*

(c) model **musā9ada**:

مساعده مساعدة	مساعدة	**musā9ada** *help*
محاسبات محاسبات	محاسبات	**muḥāsabāt** (pl.) *accounts*
مغادره مغادرة	مغادرة	**mughādara** *departure*

(d) model **irsāl**:

ارسال   إرسال   **irsāl** *despatch*

اداره   إدارة   **idāra** *administration*

إ ضراب   إضراب   **iḍrāb** *strike*

(e) model **intikhāb**:

انتخاب   انتخاب   **intikhāb** *election*

اشتراك   اشتراك   **ishtirāk** *participation*

انتظار   انتظار   **intiẓār** *wait(ing)*

(f) model **istikhdām**:

استخدام   استخدام   **istikhdām** *employment, recruitment*

استقبال   استقبال   **istiqbāl** *reception*

These nouns can of course form *relatives* (Unit 4) by adding ي... .
Read and write:

تعليمي   تعليمي   **ta9līmī** *educational, tutorial*

الاشتراكيين الاشتراكيين   الاشتراكيين   **al-ishtirākīyīn** *the socialists*

Abstract Nouns

3 You will also find *abstract* nouns (i.e. nouns denoting a quality or
state) ending in ية... -īya. These are in fact feminine relatives, but used
only as nouns. ***Read and write***, and remember if you can, such useful
abstracts as:

الاشتراكية الاشتراكية   الاشتراكية   **al-ishtirākīya** *socialism*

الدّموقراطية الدّموقراطية   الدّموقراطية   **ad-dimuqrāṭīya** *democracy*

Other Written Styles

4 Just as in our alphabet, so in the Arabic alphabet there are various
styles or typefaces in use. Here are all the letter families, first in the style

used in this book; then in a newspaper style; then in typewriting; then in
two decorative styles used on buildings and monuments:

اءبب جج درسس صص ط ععع ع فف ق كك لل مم نن ههه ه و يي ي

اءبب جج درسس صص ط ععع ع فـف ق كك لل مم نن ههه ه ويي ي

ا ٴببجج درسں صەط عمع ع فـنـق كك لل مم نـن هههه و يي ى

اءبب جج درسس صص ط ععع ع فـد ق كك لل مم نن ههه ه ويي ٮي

اءبب جج درسس صص ط ععع ع فف ق كك لل مم نن هههه ه ويي ي

Many Arabs use a handwriting style with abbreviated shapes for certain
dotted letters standing at the end of a word or alone. Reading this kind of
handwriting is much easier if we know these shapes. Here are the
important ones:

ن ‌‌‌ ق و   ض ص   ش س

Exercise 3 Read aloud these verbal nouns:

تجديد *renewal*, استقلال *independence*, تدريس *instruction*,
اجتماع *meeting*, إصلاح *reform*, تمويل *financing*, مناسبة *occasion*,
انتقال *transfer*

The answers to this exercise are immediately below.

Answers to Exercises

Exercise 1 (a) wārid, ṭālib, kāmil, 9ārif

(c) muḥāfiẓ, muqābil

(f) musta9mil, musta'jir, mustathmir

The last vowel is **i**, since from their meaning the participles are active.

Exercise 2 maksūr, mustankar, musallaḥ, muqtaraḥ

Exercise 3 tajdīd, istiqlāl, tadrīs, ijtimā9, iṣlāḥ, tamwīl, munāsaba,
intiqāl

Tests

1   These are words which we have not studied. Pronounce each one
     and identify it either as a masculine active participle or a verbal
     noun. Don't worry about the meaning; it is the form that counts:

(a) تقديم   (b) راكب   (c) مراسل

(d) إنذار   (e) مستعلم   (f) شامل

(g) افتتاح   (h) سامع   (j) مدرس

(k) استثمار

2   Write:

(a) **munāsiba**   (b) **intikhābī**   (c) **muqarrirīn**

(d) **9ummāl**   (e) **tanẓīm**

3   Here are five active participles. Give the corresponding verbal
     nouns. Read aloud and translate the participles and verbal nouns:

(a) مفتّش   (b) مشترك   (c) مرسل

(d) مساعد   (e) مستقبل

4   Read aloud:

(a) الاستقبال   (b) مدرسة للبنات

(c) مصر والعراق   (d) ايرانه

(e) القاهرة

Review

Participles and verbal nouns are forms which you will see in
abundance on signs and the like. Being able to identify such words
will help you to pronounce correctly, and to write down for future
use, many new ones which you will meet. Working out their meaning
will also be easier.

We have finished our study of separate words. We now move on to
expressions ('structures') containing two or more words, very many
of these words being like the ones you have just studied.

9

In this unit you will learn
- more about masculine and feminine nouns,
- the first basic structure, linking a noun and an adjective,
- the possessive.

New Words: المواصلات al-muwāṣalāt *Communications*

1
Essential Vocabulary

أجنبي أجانب	ajnabī ajānib *foreign*	راديو	rādiō *radio*
إصدار	iṣdār *issue, issuing*	رسالة	risāla *letter*
إعلان	i9lān *anouncement, notice, advertisement*	رسمي	rasmī *official*
		شخصي	<u>sh</u>akhṣī *personal*
بلاد بلدان	bilād buldān *country*	صورة صور	ṣūra ṣuwar *picture, photograph*
تجارة	tijāra *trade*		
تليفزيون	tilivizyūn *television*	طويل طوال	ṭawīl ṭiwāl *long*
جديد جدد	jadīd judud *new*	علاقات	9alāqāt *relations*
جميل	jamīl *beautiful*	قصير قصار	qaṣīr qiṣār *short*
حكومة	hukūma *government*	ممتاز	mumtāz *excellent*

Reference Vocabulary

بريد	barīd *mail*	لغة	lu<u>gh</u>a *language*
تقديم	taqdīm *presentation*	مجتهد	mujtahid *hardworking*
جوّي	jawwī *air (adjective)*	مجلة	majalla *magazine*
حديث حداث	hadī<u>th</u> hidā<u>th</u> *modern*	محلي	maḥallī *local*
خطاب أخطبة	<u>kh</u>iṭāb a<u>kh</u>ṭiba *speech*	مراسل	murāsil *correspondent*
زميل زملاء	zamīl zumalā' *colleague (m.)*	معرض معارض ma9riḍ ma9āriḍ *exhibition*	
صحافة	ṣiḥāfa *press*	مقالة	maqāla *(press) article*
صحفي	ṣuḥufī *journalist*	ملوّن	mulawwan *coloured*
صحيفة صحف*	ṣaḥīfa ṣuḥuf *newspaper*	مندوب	mandūb *delegate*
		مؤتمر	mu'tamar *conference*
قراءة	qirā'a *(act of) reading*	نص نصوص	naṣṣ nuṣūṣ *text*

* If you take to speaking your Arabic (and why not?) use the popular spoken word for 'newspaper', جريدة جرائد **jarīda jarā'id**. The word صحيفة is used only in writing.

Basic Structures, 1: The Description

2　Write these two words:

إعلان اعلان　**i9lān** *announcement*

هامّ هامّ　**hāmm** *important*

إعلان is a *noun.* هامّ is an *adjective.* (Look back to Unit 4, paragraph 4 for these terms, if you need to.) Now write the two words together, *noun first.* We get the expression

إعلان هامّ اعلان هامّ　*an important announcement*

This type of expression is our first basic structure, which we can call a **description**. It is very common, and in any Arab town you will see examples all around you in advertisements, notices and the like.

You will remember that Arabic has no word for *a* or *an.* Note also that, in contrast to the English, the Arabic adjective *follows* the noun.

Now *read and write* a few more descriptions (remember that relatives - Unit 4 - can be used as adjectives):

كاتب لبناني كاتب لبناني　*a Lebanese writer*

خطاب طويل خطاب طويل　**khiṭāb ṭawīl** *a long speech*

مقرّر مشغول مقرّر مشغول　(**muqarrir**) *a busy reporter*

إعلان عامّ اعلان عامّ　*a public notice*

صحفي مصري صحفي مصري　(**ṣuḥufī**) *an Egyptian journalist*

Now *read and write* an Egyptian (woman) journalist. Watch what happens to the adjective:

صحفية مصرية صحفية مصرية　*an Egyptian journalist*

The adjective assumes the feminine form too; it is said to *agree* with the feminine noun. *Read and write* an Egyptian newspaper:

صحيفة مصرية ‎صحيفة مصرية‎ (ṣaḥīfa)

In English, we generally apply the concept of masculine or feminine only
to nouns denoting people or higher animals (one possible exception
being *she* for a ship or a boat); we regard other nouns as *it* or *neuter*.
Arabic has no neuter; *all* nouns, including those for things, places and
ideas, are either masculine or feminine (صحيفة, shown above, is
feminine). For our purposes, the rules for Arabic nouns are simple:

■ nouns for male people and male animals are masculine; nouns for
   female people and female animals are feminine,

■ nouns ending in ة denoting things, places and ideas are feminine;
   nouns (with any ending) denoting towns, and most countries, are
   also feminine. Other nouns for things, places and ideas are
   masculine.

(There is a handful of exceptions, none important enough to concern us.)

With this in mind, *read and write* this series of feminine descriptions:

صحيفة مشغولة ‎صحيفة مشغولة‎ *a busy newswoman*

رسالة رسمية ‎رسالة رسمية‎ risāla rasmīya *an official letter*

صورة جميلة ‎صورة جميلة‎ ṣūra jamīla *a beautiful picture*

صحيفة عربية ‎صحيفة عربية‎ *an Arabic newspaper*

All the examples given so far have been indefinite. How do we make a
definite description? Given that we make the adjective agree with the
noun in gender (m. or f.), it is logical that we make it agree *in definition*
too, i.e. indefinite adjective for an indefinite noun, definite adjective for a
definite noun. We do just that. *Read and write:*

الكاتب اللبناني ‎الكاتب اللبناني‎ *the Lebanese writer* (m.)

المقرّر المشغول ‎المقرّر المشغول‎ *the busy reporter* (m.)

النصّ الطويل ‎النصّ الطويل‎ (an-naṣṣ) *the long text* (m.)

الصحافة الغربية ‎الصحافة الغربية‎ aṣ-ṣiḥāfa l-gharbīya*
the western press (f.)

الرسالة الطويلة الرساله الطويله   **ar-risāla ṭ-ṭawīla***
the long letter (f.)

المجلة الجديدة المجلّة الجديده   **al-majalla l-jadīda***
the new magazine (f.)

We apply to adjectives the same rules for adding the article ...اـل
(assimilation to sun letters etc., Units 2 and 3) as for nouns.

* Remember that the 'weak' **a-** of the article is dropped after a vowel. It is easiest to pronounce the vowelless article as part of the preceding word: **as-siḥāfa l-gharbīya** (etc.).

A proper name (*Egypt, Ahmad*) is always definite, even if it has no article. So a description with a proper name has a definite adjective, just like *Alexander the Great* or *Ivan the Terrible* in English. Read and write:

مصر الحديثة مصر الحديثه   (**al-ḥadītha**) *modern Egypt* (f.)

Exercise 1 Make as many meaningful descriptions as possible, using a noun from list (a) and an adjective (making it agree) from list (b). Read and translate your descriptions:

(a) الإعلان، صحيفة، بلاد، الصورة، رسالة

(b) هامّ، مفيد، شخصي، طويل، محلي، جميل

Exercise 2 Read and translate these newspaper headings. Which descriptions are masculine, and which feminine? Definite or indefinite?

The answers to these exercises follow paragraph 5 below.

3 So far all the descriptions have been singular. Descriptions can also be dual (though by their nature these are rare). The adjective agrees, forming its dual in the same manner as the noun. The description can be indefinite or definite. *Read and write:*

مقرّرين غربيين مقرّرين غربيين
مقرّران غربيان مقرّران غربيان

} *two western*
reporters (m.)

الرّسالتين الرّسميتين الرّسالتين الرّسميتين **ar-risālatayn**
ar-rasmīyatayn *both (the) official letters* (f.)
(also الرّسالتان الرّسميتان **ar-risālatān ar-rasmīyatān**)

4 As you would expect, plural descriptions, both indefinite and definite, also exist. They occur very frequently.

In a plural description, the noun forms its plural in one of the three ways we have studied in Unit 7 (feminine regular, masculine regular, and the irregular forms).

But the adjective forms its plural in one of these three ways *only when it describes people*. We call this the **animate plural** form.

When the adjective describes any other plural noun (animals, things, places, ideas) it always has the same form as the *feminine singular*, irrespective of whether the noun is masculine or feminine. We call this the **inanimate plural** form.

This is a most important rule, and you will see it in action countless times.

Inanimate Plural Rule: *An adjective describing a plural noun which denotes anything other than people is put into the inanimate plural form, which is always the same as the feminine singular.*

Read and write these plural descriptions; note the form of the adjective in each case (an. = animate, inan. = inanimate):

زملاء ممتازين\ون زملاء ممتازين (ون...) **zumalā' mumtāzīn** (-ūn)

زميلات ممتازات زميلات ممتازات **zamīlāt mumtāzāt**
excellent colleagues (f. an. pl.)

اقتراحات ممتازه   اقتراحات ممتازة   **iqtirāḥāt mumtāza**
excellent proposals (inan. pl.)

مقالات ممتازه   مقالات ممتازة   **maqālāt mumtāza**
excellent articles (inan. pl.)

Remember that the choice between animate pl. and inanimate pl. (= f. sing.) forms arises only for the *adjective*, not the noun. And then only for the *plural*, not the singular or the dual.

Here are more plural descriptions, of various kinds, including a mixture of definite and indefinite (but remember that, since Arabic uses the article for any noun used to cover a whole category in general, you may not always want to express the article in English). Spot the animate plural and inanimate plural adjectives too. Read and write:

بلدان غربيه   بلدان غربية   (buldān)   *western countries*

صور ملوّنه   صور ملوّنة   **ṣuwar mulawwana**
colour(ed) photographs

ممثلين اجانب   ممثلين أجانب   (ajānib)
foreign representatives

الصحف الأجنبيه   الصحف الأجنبية   **aṣ-ṣuḥuf al-'ajnabīya**
(the) foreign newspapers

الكمبيوترات اليابانيه   الكمبيوترات اليابانية
(the) Japanese computers

مندوبين يابانيين   مندوبين يابانيين   (mandūbīn)
Japanese delegates

اعلانات حكوميه   إعلانات حكومية
government announcements

زميلات مجتهدات   زميلات مجتهدات   (mujtahidāt)
hard-working colleagues (f.)

Possessive

5   In English the so-called *possessive* (more correctly, possessive adjective) is a word: *my, your, his, her, its, our, your, their.* In Arabic it is an ending added to the word denoting what is possessed. Write *colleague* in Arabic, indefinite masculine form:

زميل   زميل

Now add the ending ي... -ī and you get *my colleague* (m.):

زَمِيلِي   زميلي   zamīlī

A final ة on the possessed noun changes to ت (since ة can stand only at the end of a word) before the possessive ending is added. Write *my car*:

سَيّارَتِي   سيارتي   sayyāratī

Here are the possessive endings for all the persons we need, including *my* which we have just studied:

ي...	-ī	*my*	نا...	-na	*our*
ك...	-ak	*your* (m.)	كم...	-kum	*your* (pl.)
ك...	-ik	*your* (f.)			
ه...	-u, -hu	*his, its* (m.)	هم...	-hum	*their* (animate pl.)
ها...	-ha	*her, its* (f.), *their* (inanimate pl.)			

These are all added to the indefinite noun in the same way as ي... .
Read and write:

تَقْرِيرِي   تقريري   **taqrīrī** *my report*

مُشْكِلَتِي   مشكلتي   **mushkilatī** *my problem*

اِقْتِرَاحَك   اقتراحك   **iqtirāḥak,** …**ik** *your proposal*

لَجْنَتَك   لجنتك   **lajnatak,** …**ik** *your committee*

مَكْتَبُه   مكتبه   **maktabu** *his office*

صُورَتُه   صورته   **ṣūratu** *his, its picture*

اِسْمُها   اسمها   **ismhā** *her, its, their* (inan.) *name*

اِحْتِجَاجُنا   احتجاجنا   **iḥtijājna** *our objection*

مَجَلّتُنا   مجلتنا   **majallatna** *our magazine*

وُصُولُكُم   وصولكم   **wusūlkum** *your* (pl.) *arrival*

زيارتكم   زيارتكم   **ziyāratkum** *your* (pl.) *visit*

إعلانهم   اعلانهم   **i9lānhum** *their advertisement*

طائرتهم   طائرتهم   **ṭā'irathum** *their aeroplane*

Certain things need explaining:

- ■ The possessive *you* shown above has three forms: one used when the 'possessor' is a male person, one used when the possessor is a female person, and one used when the possessors constitute a group.

- ■ We use the possessive **-u** or **-hu** when the possessor would be expressed with a masculine noun; we have to translate with *his* or *its* as appropriate.

- ■ We use the possessive **-ha** when the possessor would be expressed with a feminine noun, *or a plural noun not denoting people* (this is the inanimate plural again); we have to translate with *her*, *its* or *their* as appropriate.

- ■ We use the possessive **-hum** *their* only when the possessors are people, i.e. animate.

- ■ No dual? Yes, there are dual possessives (= *of you both, of them both*), but they are so rarely used that we need not learn them, and they have been left out of this table.

When a noun has a possessive ending attached, it logically becomes definite. So any accompanying adjective has the article. Read and write:

مكتبي الجديد   مكتبي الجديد   **maktabī l-jadīd**
my new office

لزيارتك الرسمية   لزيارتك الرسمية   **li-ziyāratak ar-rasmīya**
for your official visit

منظمته الصغيرة   منظمته الصغيرة   **munaẓẓamatu ṣ-ṣaghīra**
his small organisation

إنتاجهم الصناعي   إنتاجهم الصناعي   **intājhum aṣ-ṣinā9ī**
their industrial production

We can also add these possessives to a noun with the regular plural noun ending ...ات , or to an irregular plural. *Read and write:*

معلوماتهم المفيدة **ma9lūmāthum al-mufīda**
their useful information

مشاكلنا الفنّية **mashākilna l-fannīya**
our technical problems

Adding a possessive to a noun with the dual ending, or with the regular plurals ...ين\...ون **-īn/ūn**, involves various changes which are frankly not worth our trouble, since these forms are very rarely found with possessives. We can ignore them.

Exercise 3 Who placed advertisement (a)? And what is the firm which placed advertisement (b) looking for? (Read only the big print!):

Exercise 4 Read and translate the following descriptions:

(a) صور ملوّنة   (b) للمقرّرين الأجانب   (c) منظّمتنا الفنّية
(d) الصحافة المحلّية والوطنية   (e) مكتبك الجديد

The answers to these exercises are given immediately below.

Answers to Exercises

Exercise 1

الإعلان الهامّ\المفيد\الشخصي\الطويل\المحلي\الجميل **al-'i9lān**
al-hāmm, al-mufīd, ash-shakhṣī, aṭ-ṭawīl, al-maḥallī, al-jamīl
the important, useful, personal, long, local, beautiful announcement/advertisement

صحيفة هامّة\مفيدة\محلّية **ṣaḥīfa hāmma, mufīda, maḥallīya**
an important, a useful, local newspaper

بلاد هامّ\جميل **bilad hāmm, jamīl** *an important, a beautiful country*

الصورة الهامّة\المفيدة\الشخصية\الجميلة **aṣ-ṣūra l-hāmma,**
l-mufīda, sh-shakhṣīya, l-jamīla *the important, useful, personal (private), beautiful picture/photograph*

رسالة هامّة\مفيدة\شخصية\طويلة\جميلة risāla hāmma, mufīda, <u>sh</u>akhṣīya, ṭawīla, jamīla *an important, a useful, private, long, beautiful letter*

Exercise 2 (a) **i9lān ḥukūmī** *Government(al) Announcement/Notice*, indefinite masculine

(b) **at-tijāra l-waṭanī** *('The') National Trade*, definite feminine

(c) **īṭāliya l-jamīla** *Beautiful Italy ('Italy the Beautiful')*, definite feminine

(d) **inti<u>kh</u>āb hāmm** *an important election*, indefinite masculine

Exercise 3 (a) **al-<u>kh</u>uṭūṭ al-jawwīya l-waṭanīya** *('The') National Airlines ('Air Lines')*

(b) **mumaththilīn fannīyīn** *Technical Representatives*

Exercise 4 (a) **ṣuwar mulawwana** *coloured pictures/photographs*

(b) **li-l-muqarrirīn al-'ajānib** *for ('the') foreign reporters*

(c) **munaẓẓamatna l-fannīya** *our technical organisation*

(d) **aṣ-ṣiḥāfa l-maḥallīya wa l-waṭanīya** *the local and national press*

(e) **maktabak al-jadīd** *your new office*

Tests

1 Read aloud and translate:

(a) صحافتنا الأسبوعية　　(b) احتجاجاتهم الطويلة

(c) الزَّملاء الفنّيين　　(d) صحف عربية

(e) بنك أجنبي

2 Put adjective and noun together in a description, changing the adjective as necessary:

(a) مدرسة، ابتدائي　　(b) المطر، وطني

(c) تقاريره، يومي　　(d) لزوّارنا، أجنبي

(e) انتخابات، عامّ

3 Make these descriptions plural:

(a) رسالة طويلة　　(b) التقرير الفنّي

(c) مُمثّل أجنبي　　(d) الطائرة الأميركية

(e) خطّ جوّي

Review

An important step. Once you have mastered this unit, you have broken through the barrier separating single words from meaningful expressions. And you have done your first manipulations in the language.

The words are hard, and there are too many to remember at a first attempt. Concentrate on the essential vocabulary; but don't hesitate to look up any word at all if you are uncertain.

10

In this unit you will learn
■ the personal pronouns,
■ the second basic structure, making simple statements.

New Words: العمل al-9amal *Work*

1   *Essential Vocabulary*

تاجر تجّار **tājir tujjār** *trader*	مأمور **ma'mūr** *public official*
خبير خبراء **khabīr khubarā'** *expert*	مدني **madanī** *civil, urban*
دولي **duwalī** *international*	مشهور **mashhūr** *famous*
صعب صعاب **ṣa9b ṣi9āb** *difficult*	مهندس **muhandis** *engineer*
طبيب أطبّاء **ṭabīb aṭibbā'** *doctor*	موجود **moujūd** *present* (not absent)
عالمي **9ālamī** *world(wide)*	موظف **muwaẓẓaf** *employee*
غائب **ghā'ib** *absent*	وكالة **wikāla** *agency*

Reference Vocabulary

أجر أجور **ajr ujūr** *wage*	ممرّض\ممرّضة **mumarriḍ(a)** *nurse*
بطالة **baṭāla** *unemployment*	هندسة **handasa** *engineering*
راتب رواتب **rātib rawātib** *salary*	واضح **wāḍiḥ** *clear*
سمسار سماسير **simsār samāsīr** *broker*	وظيفة وظائف **waẓīfa**
شغل أشغال **shughl ashghāl** *work, job*	**waẓā'if** *job, post*
عمل أعمال **9amal a9māl** *work, labour*	وكيل وكلاء **wakīl**
معقول **ma9qūl** *reasonable*	**wukalā'** *agent*
مقبول **maqbūl** *acceptable*	

Personal pronouns

2   In previous units we have seen most of the personal pronouns ('I, you, he' etc.) . It may be helpful to have them clearly set out, with one we haven't seen so far. Write them out:

أنا ا أنا ana *I*   نحن نحن naḥnu *we*

أنت انت anta *you* (m.)   أنتم انتم antum *you* (pl.)

أنت انت anti *you* (f.)

هو هو huwa *he, it* (m.)   هم هم hum *they* (people)

هي هي hiya *she, it,* (f.), *they* (other than people, i.e. inanimate pl.)

These pronouns correspond exactly to the possessives given in Unit 9, paragraph 5. The notes given there apply here as well.

Basic Structures, 2: The Equation

3 You probably didn't realise that you can already read and write whole sentences in Arabic. Well, you can. ***Read and write*** these ones:

هو مسؤول.   هو مسؤول. (mas'ūl)
He is responsible.

هو مهندس.   هو مهندس. (muhandis)
He is an engineer.

زميله مسؤول.   زميله مسؤول. (zamīlu)
His colleague is responsible.

زميله طبيب.   زميله طبيب.
His colleague is a doctor.

زميله صحفي مصري. زميله صحفي مصري. *His colleague is an Egyptian journalist.*

It is as simple as that. Whereas in English we need a verb form 'is' for such a sentence, Arabic needs nothing beyond the two parts of the statement. These Arabic sentences are complete and correct.

(English uses this verbless structure also, but only in newspaper headlines and the like: *"Dollar Devalued", "Chairman Dismissed", "Farmers Furious".*)

We can call this structure an **equation**, because, like a mathematical equation such as '$x = 2$', both parts are regarded as equal to each other. The equation is the second of the three basic structures which we study. We can use any pronoun in the first part of the equation.
Read and write:

أنا مسؤول. انا مسؤول. *I am responsible.*

هي مسؤولة.   *She is responsible.*

(mashhūra) هي طبيبة مشهورة.
She is a famous doctor.

> **Equation Rule:** *In a simple statement, Arabic does not use any verb form corresponding to the English 'am, is, are'. The verb is simply omitted.*

You will notice that the second part has to agree with the first part. Also, we can of course have a noun instead of a pronoun. For both, we observe the *inanimate plural rule* (Unit 9, paragraph 4) throughout. *Read and write*, with an eye on the inanimate plural:

(sa9ba) المشكلة صعبة.   *The problem is difficult.* (feminine singular)

المشاكل صعبة   *The problems are difficult.* (inanimate plural)

(al-iqtirāḥāt) الاقتراحات طويلة.   *The proposals are long.*

hiya ṭawīla. هي طويلة.   *They (the proposals) are long.*

When we have to use a masculine regular plural ending in an equation, it takes the form ون... -ūn (not ين...-īn); when we use a dual, it takes the form ان... -ān (not ين...-ayn). *Read and write:*

المفتّشون مسؤولون.   *The inspectors are responsible.*

المفتّشان مسؤولان.   *Both inspectors are responsible.*

(masrūrūn) نحن مسرورون.   *We are pleased.*

> **Exercise 1** Make as many meaningful equations as possible, taking your first part from list (a) and your second part from list (b). The words must be used as they are; don't change their form:
>
> (a) اقتراحاتنا، هي، الرئيس، المندوبون، الصحفي
>
> (b) موجودون، مقبولة، موجود، واضحة، عراقي

Exercise 2 Translate into Arabic and read your answer aloud:

(a) *The engineer is Lebanese.*   (b) *They are Italians.*

(c) *The minister is absent.*   (d) *The doctor is German.*

(e) *She is a foreign doctor.*

The answers to these exercises follow paragraph 4 below.

We have said that the second part of the equation must agree with the first part. This is only partly true. Look back at the equations quoted so far, especially the ones beginning with a noun. Can you see any way in which the second part does *not* agree with the first part?

Here is a clue. ***Read and write*** this expression, which bears some resemblance to one of the equations we have already written:

المشكلة الصعبة   المشكلة الصعبة   al-mushkila ṣ-ṣa9ba

You see the difference. What we have here is not an equation at all, but a *description* (Unit 9): *'the difficult problem'*. In a description the adjective agrees with the noun in every possible way, including indefinite/definite. The equations we have written earlier in this paragraph have a definite first part but an *indefinite* second part.

We can have equations with a definite second part. But they almost always have a pronoun in the first part. ***Read and write:***

هو الرئيس. هو الرئيس .   (ar-ra'īs) He is the chairman.

هم الخبراء. هم الخبراء .   They are the experts.

If the meaning of the equation demands a noun in the first part, then we use the noun but we re-state it with its corresponding pronoun.
Read and write:

العراقي هو الرئيس. العراقي هو الرئيس   The Iraqi ('he') is
                                          the chairman.

زملائي هم الخبراء. زملائي هم الخبراء .   My colleagues ('they')
                                          are the experts.

Adding the pronoun makes it impossible to read the expression as a description. It must be an equation. But such equations are comparatively rare. Equations of the type we have studied earlier in the paragraph, with an *indefinite* second part, are much more common.

4 Equations with descriptions

Either part of an equation can itself be a description. As long as the relationship between the two parts is respected, the equation is still correct. Look back at the fifth and eighth examples in paragraph 3 above:

زميله صحفي مصري.   هي طبيبة مشهورة.

in which the second part consists of a description. We can have the first part as a description; or indeed both parts. If the equation begins to look a little heavy or complicated, the writer may break it up by adding the corresponding pronoun to the first part, showing clearly which part is which. We can always do this, with any equation. ***Read and write:***

المهندس المدني موجود.

al-muhandis al-mādanī moujūd.
The civil engineer is present.

المندوب العربي هو مهندس مدني.

The Arab delegate ('he')
is a civil engineer.

Exercise 3 Read and translate these newspaper headings; then answer the questions:

(a) المؤتمر الدولي مفتوح

(b) "البنوك مسؤولة."

(c) وظيفة هامّة وصعبة

(d) الوزير الجديد مريض

(e) لبنان تاجر عالمي

Which ones are equations and which are descriptions? Which equations (if any) contain a description?

Exercise 4 Read aloud and translate:

(a) الطبيب إنجليزي.

(b) الاقتراحات معقولة.

(c) هو خبير فني.

(d) مصر كبيرة.

(e) اقتراحنا جديد.

The answers to these exercises are given immediately below.

Answers to Exercises

Exercise 1 اقتراحاتنا مقبولة\واضحة. iqtirāḥātna maqbūla/wāḍiḥa.
Our proposals are acceptable/clear.

هي مقبولة\واضحة. hiya maqbula/wāḍiḥa.
It is / They are acceptable/clear.

الرئيس موجود\عراقي. ar-ra'īs moujūd /9irāqī.
The chairman is present /Iraqi.

المندوبون موجودون. al-mandūbūn moujūdūn.
The delegates are present.

الصحفي موجود\عراقي. aṣ-ṣuḥufī moujūd /9irāqī.
The journalist is present /Iraqi.

Exercise 2 (a) المهندس لبناني. al-muhandis lubnānī.

(b) هم إطاليون. hum īṭālīyūn.   (c) الوزير غائب. al-wazīr ghā'ib.

(d) الطبيب ألماني. aṭ-ṭabīb almānī.

(e) هي طبيبة أجنبية. hiya ṭabība ajnabīya.

Exercise 3 (a) al-mu'tamar ad-duwalī maftūḥ. *The international conference is open.* Equation with a definite description as first part.

(b) al-bunūk mas'ūla. *The banks are responsible.* Equation.

(c) waẓīfa hāmma wa-ṣa9ba *An important and difficult job.* Not an equation but an indefinite description.

(d) al-wazīr al-jadīd marīḍ. *The new minister is ill.* Equation with a definite description as first part.

(e) lubnān tājir 9ālamī. *Lebanon is a world trader.* Equation with an indefinite description as second part.

Exercise 4 (a) **aṭ-ṭabīb ingilīzī.** *The doctor is British/English.*
(b) **al-iqtirāḥāt ma9qūla.** *The proposals are reasonable.*
(c) **huwa khabīr fannī.** *He is a technical expert.*
(d) **miṣr kabīra.** *Egypt is big.*
(e) **iqtirāḥna jadīd.** *Our proposal is new.*

Tests

1   Read aloud and translate:

(a) وظيفته صعبة.

(b) المؤتمر التجاري هامّ.

(c) الوزراء موجودون.

(d) الصورة جميلة.

(e) الصورة الجميلة

2   Put the words together in an equation, making any necessary
changes. Read aloud your answer and translate it:

(a) موظّفون؛ مسرور.

(b) مطارنا، دولي؛ هامّ.

(c) هو؛ تاجر، دولي.

(d) النصّ؛ واضح، ومقبول.

(e) مأمور؛ مشغول.

3   Fill in the missing letter. Read aloud and translate the word:

(a) و...يفة

(b) مـ...ظّف

(c) مـ...دوب

(d) غا...ب

(e) الخـ..راء

Review

With an understanding of *descriptions* studied in the last unit and
equations studied in this unit, you have made a serious step towards
being able to read and understand the headings of many notices and
announcements, and many newspaper headlines. There remains a
third basic structure, also related to these two. But before we tackle
that one, we should arm ourselves with some important prepositions
(*to, from, in, with* and the like), which come in the next unit.

11

In this unit you will learn

- ■ important prepositions,
- ■ the command form of the verb,
- ■ a form of equation often used in signs.

New Words: البلد al-balad *Town*

1   *Essential Vocabulary - Prepositions*

إلى	**ila** *to*	في	**fī** *in*
ب	**bi-** *with, by, in*	قبل	**qabl** *before*
بعد	**ba9d** *after*	ل	**li-** *to, for, of*
على	**9ala** *on*	مع	**ma9** *with*
عن	**9an** *from, about*	من	**min** *from*

Essential Vocabulary - Other words

إشارة	**ishāra** *sign*	مرور	**murūr**(also:)
إيقاف	**īqāf** *parking*		*passing, turning*
بلد بلاد	**balad bilād** *town*	مفرق مفارق	**mafraq mafāriq**
بوليس	**būlīs** *police*		*crossroad*
تدخين	**tadkhīn** *smoking*	ممنوع	**mamnū9** *prohibited*
توقيف	**touqīf** *parking*	ميدان ميادين	**maydān mayādīn**
حدّ حدود	**ḥadd ḥudūd** *limit*		*square*
سرعة	**sur9a** *speed*	نقل	**naql** *transport*
طريق طرق	**ṭarīq ṭuruq** *road*	وقوف	**wuqūf** *stopping*
كراج\جراج	**garāj** *garage*	يسار	**yasār** *left(-hand)*
كيلومتر\كم	**kīlomitr** *kilometre*	يمين	**yamīn** *right(-hand)*
مدينة مدن	**madīna mudun** *city*		

Reference Vocabulary - Prepositions

أمام	**amām** *in front of*	خلال	**khilāl** *during*
تحت	**taht** *below, under*	داخل	**dākhil** *inside*
حسب	**ḥasab** *according to*	دون\بدون	**dūn, bidūn** *without*
خارج	**khārij** *outside*	ضدّ	**ḍidd** *against*

غير **ghayr** *apart from*   ك\مثل **ka-, mithl** *like, as*

فوق **fouq** *above, over*   وراء **warā'** *behind, beyond*

Reference Vocabulary - Other words

برلمان **barlamān** *parliament*   قصر قصور **qaṣr quṣūr** *palace*

بلدية **baladīya** *town hall*   قنصلية **qunṣulīya** *consulate*

جامعة **jāmi9a** *university*   مجلس مجالس **majlis majālis** *council*

شرطي **shurṭī** *policeman*   مركز مراكز **markaz marākiz** *centre*

عاصمة عواصم **9āṣima 9awāṣim** *capital city*

2 Prepositions

A preposition is a word connecting a noun or pronoun with the rest of
the sentence. Examples in English are *in, with, from*. In the essential and
reference vocabularies given above the prepositions are shown
separately because of their importance.

In Arabic the preposition precedes its noun, as it does in English. ***Read
and write:***

بعد سنه   بعد سنة   **ba9d sana** *after a year*

ضدّ الحكومه   ضدّ الحكومة   **(ḍidd)** *against the government*

حسب الخبراء   حسب الخبراء   **(ḥasab)** *according to the experts*

داخل البلاد   داخل البلاد   **(dākhil)** *inside the country*

في **fī** shortens its vowel, becoming **fi** in pronunciation before an article.
The spelling is unchanged. ***Read and write***, comparing the sounds:

في بنك   في بنك   **fī bank** *in a bank* (long ī)

في البنك   في البنك   **fi l-bank** *in the bank* (short i)

When we want to combine a preposition with a *pronoun*, we add the
pronoun as an ending, using the same endings as the possessives (Unit 9,
paragraph 5). The meanings then become *me, you, him* etc. We can add
the pronoun endings to the prepositions which end in a consonant
(including **hamza**) without further ado. ***Read and write:***

معي ma9ī *with me*   أمامه امامه amāmu *in front of him*

The prepositions ending in a vowel, long or short, are unfortunately not so simple. Details are given below. Don't try to learn the following details at one stroke. Use them for reference until at least some become familiar. Some of the explanation concerns only pronunciation anyway, which is not our main target.

- إلى ila and على 9ala change to ...إليـ ilay- and ...عليـ 9alay- before adding a pronoun. *Read and write:*

إليها اليها ilayha *to her, it, them* (inanimate pl.)

علينا علينا alayna *up to us ('on us')*

You have certainly heard of the classic greeting السَّلام عليكم as-salām 9alaykum *Peace (be) upon you.* Thinking of this might help you to remember how these two prepositions change before a pronoun.

- ل li- (you will recall that one-letter words are written together with the next word) becomes لي lī for 'for me', but changes to la- before any other pronoun. *Read and write:*

له ل lahu *for him, it*   لهم لهم lahum *for them*

- After ب bi-, ...إليـ ilay- and ...عليـ 9alay- (see above), the pronoun ending ...ه is pronounced -hi, and ...هم is pronounced -him. The spelling is unchanged. *Read and write:*

به به bihi *with him/it, in him/it*   إليهم اليهم ilayhim *to them*

3 Prepositions in Equations

We can use a phrase consisting of preposition + noun, or preposition + pronoun, as either part of an equation, without further formality. *Read and write:*

هو ضدّ الاقتراح. هو ضدّ الاقتراح.   *He is against the proposal.*

الطبيب في البلد.* الطبيب في البلد.   *The doctor is in ('the') town.*

المرور إلى اليسار ممنوع. المرورالى اليسار ممنوع .

al-murur ila l-yasār mamnū9.

NO LEFT TURN ('*Turning left prohibited*')

* No 'helping' pronoun (Unit 10, paragraph 3) is needed here. The preposition makes the equation clear and unmistakable.

4 Translating prepositions

Arabic phrases do not always have the preposition which exactly corresponds to the English; be prepared for different ones. Here are two examples out of many. *Read and write:*

مسؤول عن   مـــؤول عن   **(9an)** *responsible for*

ممنون من   ممنون من   **(min)** *grateful for*

5 Command Form

You may see a notice or instruction like one of these. *Read and write:*

اشرب فانتا اشرب فانتا   **ishrab fanta** *Drink Fanta*

اقفل الباب اقفل الباب   **(iqfil)** *Shut the Door*

اركب\انزل هنا اركب\انزل هنا   **irkab/inzil huna** *Get on/off here*

افتح بانتباه افتح بانتباه   **iftaḥ bī-ntibāh** *Open carefully*

انظر ..   انظر ...   **unẓur** *See ...*

اطلب ...   اطلب ...   **uṭlub** *Ask for ...*

These are verbs, in the command form. They can often be recognised by two characteristics: they stand at the beginning of the expression, as in English; and they begin with **alif**, which is pronounced **i-**, **u-** or **a-** depending on the verb.

Unfortunately not all commands take this easily recognisable form. In Unit 3 we had تمهّل **tamahhal** *SLOW DOWN*, and in Unit 6 قف **qif** *STOP*. These important notices are also in the command form.

All the forms shown here are masculine, which is the form generally used;

you may occasionally see the plural form (as if addressing a group), which adds و‍ا... pronounced -ū (the alif is silent):

اشربوا i‍sh‍rabū *Drink*; ... اطلبوا uṭlubū *Ask for* ... (etc.)

These forms are used in advertisements, or when an authoritative tone (police, road signs, warnings of danger etc.) is needed. A more polite form, similar to our *Please* ... takes the following guise. ***Read and write:***

الرجاء الانتظار هنا.   الرجاءالانتظار هنا.   ar-rajā'
al-intiẓar huna. *Please Wait Here.*

You will note that the verbal noun, in this case انتظار *waiting*, is definite in this expression.

Please do not ... is written using the noun عدم 9adam *lack of*, followed by a definite verbal noun. ***Read and write:***

الرجاء عدم التّدخين.   الرجاء عدم التدخين   ar-rajā'
9adam at-tad‍kh‍īn. *Please do not Smoke.*

6 Signs and Notices

In many road signs and similar short messages and warnings, an equation is used in reverse order, for effect. This happens, for example, with the essential word ممنوع mamnū9 *PROHIBITED*. In an ordinary text, the sentence *Entry is prohibited* would be

الدخول ممنوع. ad-du‍kh‍ūl mamnu9.

This is the normal word-order for an equation, as you have learned. But often the same sentence in a sign will read

ممنوع الدخول *NO ENTRY* ('Entry prohibited')

for special effect. Don't be surprised when you see this. It is simply an equation with its parts in reverse order.

Not all Arab countries use the same words for everything, so don't be confused if you find unfamiliar words on traffic and other signs. The words given in this book are very widely used.

Exercise 1 Read and translate these equations:

(a) الاسم فوق الإعلان. (b) المفرق خارج البلد.

(c) مكتبي أمام المستشفى. (d) الكراج على يمينك.

(e) البلدية وراءنا.

Exercise 2 Write equations with the opposite meaning of those shown in Exercise 2. Read your answers aloud.

Exercise 3 Fit the captions to the signs, one of which we know already. Read the captions aloud and translate them:

ممنوع الدخول، قف، ممنوع للمرور، المرور إلى اليسار ممنوع،
ممنوع للسيّارلت، مستشفى، ممنوع التّدخين، مفرق خطر.

The answers to these exercises are given immediately below.

Answers to Exercises

Exercise 1 (a) **al-ism fouq al-'i9lān.**

The name is above the announcement.

(b) **al-mafraq khārij al-balad.** *The crossroad is outside the town.*

(c) **maktabī amām al-mustashfa.** *My office is in front of the hospital.*

(d) **al-garāj 9ala yamīnak.** *The garage is on your right.*

(e) **al-baladīya warā'na.** *The town hall is behind us.*

Exercise 2 (a) الاسم نحت الإعلان **al-ism taḥt al-'i9lān.**

(b) المفرق داخل البلد. **al-mafraq dākhil al-balad.**

(c) مكتبي وراء المستشفى **maktabī warā' al-mustashfa.**

(d) ‏الكراخ علي يسارك.‏ al-garāj 9ala yasārak.

(e) ‏البلدية أمامنا.‏ al-baladīya amāmna.

Exercise 3 (a) ‏قف‏ qif *STOP*

(b) ‏ممنوع الدخول‏ mamnū9 ad-dukhūl *NO ENTRY*

(c) ‏ممنوع للسيّارات‏ mamnū9 li-s-sayyārāt *VEHICLES PROHIBITED*

(d) ‏ممنوع للمرور‏ mamnū9 li-l-murūr *TRAFFIC PROHIBITED*

(e) ‏المرور إلى اليسار ممنوع‏ al-murūr ila l-yasār mamnū9 *NO LEFT TURN*

(f) ‏ممنوع التّدخين‏ mamnū9 at-tadkhīn *NO SMOKING*

(g) ‏مفرق خطر‏ mafraq khaṭir *DANGEROUS CROSSROAD*

(h) ‏مستشفى‏ mustashfa *HOSPITAL*

Tests

1   Read aloud and translate:

(a) ‏ممنوع الانتظار‏   (b) ‏في البلد‏   (c) ‏في البلاد *‏

(d) ‏أشغال على الطريق‏   (e) ‏المرور إلى اليمين‏

* two possible meanings

2   Make the adjective agree with the noun or pronoun in a description:

(a) ‏سيّارات (جديد)‏   (b) ‏أشغال (هامّ)‏

(c) ‏الشرطة (محلّي)‏   (d) ‏مستشفيات (كبير)‏

(e) ‏مشاكل (فنّي)‏

3   Which of these are descriptions, and which are equations? (All full stops have been omitted, not to make things too easy.) Read everything aloud and translate it:

(a) ‏المأمور المسؤول‏   (b) ‏المأمورون هم المسؤولون‏

(c) ‏البلاد جميل‏   (d) ‏زميلي في المستشفى‏

(e) ‏زميلي المريض‏

Review

Prepositions are useful because of their function in linking words, opening up phrases which otherwise might be a problem. They are so common that they are not only worth learning; they stick in the mind more easily than many other words. And they fit into the equation structure which is at the heart of many headlines and announcements.

We go on now to our third and last basic structure.

12

In this unit you will learn

■ the third basic structure, linking two or more nouns.

New Words: الإدارة al-'idāra *Administration*

1   *Essential Vocabulary*

تأمين ta'mīn *insurance*	رخصة رخص rukhṣa rukhaṣ *licence*
تسجيل tasjīl *registration*	ضريبة ضرائب ḍarība ḍarā'ib *tax*
جمرك jumruk *customs*	عقد عقود 9aqd 9uqūd *contract*
حساب ḥisāb *account*	قسم أقسام qism aqsām *department*
دائرة دوائر dā'ira dawā'ir	نمرة نمر numra numar *number*
directorate	اليوم al-youm *today*
دفع مدفوعات daf9 madfū9āt *payment*	

Reference Vocabulary

اقتصاد iqtiṣād *economy, economics*	زراعة zirā9a *agriculture*
تربية tarbiya *education*	سياسة siyāsa *policy, politics*
خارجية khārijīya *Foreign Affairs*	مالية mālīya *Financial Affairs*
داخلية dākhilīya *Home Affairs*	نفط nafṭ *oil*
دفاع difā9 *defence*	

Basic Structures, 3: The Construct

2   Write the two nouns

مكتب   مكتب   *an office*

المدير   المدير   *the manager*

Now put these two together as they stand, and you have:

مكتب المدير مكتب المدير maktab al-mudīr *the manager's office*

Now ***read and write***:

الشركة الشركة   *the company*

Now **read and write** the company office or the company's office:

مكتب الشركة مكتب الشرك   maktab a<u>sh</u>-<u>sh</u>arika

Now **read and write** these expressions, which are exactly similar in form:

بيت المدير بيت المدير   the manager's house

عقد العمّال عقد العمّال   (9aqd) the workers' contract

شغل زميلي شغل زميلي   my colleague's work

تسجيل السيّارات تسجيل السيّارات   (tasjīl) car ('cars')
                                                    registration

طريق المطار طريق المطار   ṭarīq al-maṭār the airport road

Simply by putting two nouns together, with no other words at all, we build an association between them. The nature of this association is often possession, but not always.

This type of expression is our third basic structure; it is called a **construct**. We have to observe two simple rules in making a construct:

- the *qualifying* noun (مدير) follows the *qualified* noun (مكتب); think of the word-order of *the leg of the table*; so: *the office of the manager*.
- only the last noun can have a definite 'marker', i.e. either the article ...الـ (Units 2 and 3) or a possessive ending (Unit 9); the first noun must remain *indefinite* in form.

* Remember (Unit 2) that when a noun is used generally or universally ('cars'), Arabic makes it definite, unlike English.

Construct Rule 1: *In a construct, only the last noun can have the article or a possessive ending.*

Now **read and write** a couple of constructs with a proper name as last noun:

مكتب احمد مكتب احمد   (aḥmad) Aḥmad's office

اقتصاد مصر اقتصاد مصر   (iqtiṣād) the economy of Egypt

These are still correct: the first noun is indefinite in form, and the last noun is definite because it is a proper noun or name, which is definite by nature.

Exercise 1 Read aloud and translate the following nameplates, which are all in the form of constructs:

(a) قسم الحسابات (b) مدخل الوزارة (c) مدير المكتب

(d) قسم التسجيل (e) استقبال الزوّار (f) مكتب المدفوعات

Exercise 2 Put each pair into a construct. Read it out and translate it:

(a) مكتب، عقود (b) قسم، هندسة (c) تأمين، بيتي (d) شغل، وزارة

Exercise 3 Which way, right or left, to (a) *Traffic Department*
(b) *Tax Office* (c) *Car Registration* (d) *Issue of Licences*?
Read each direction aloud:

→ تسجيل السّيارات قسم المرور →
→ مكتب الضرائب إصدار الرخص →

The answers to these exercises follow paragraph 7 below.

When the first noun of a construct ends in ة... , this is pronounced -at. In handwriting we always write the dots of ة here. Write the word for *ministry*:

وزارة   وزارة

Now *read and write* Ministry of Labour, and note the pronunciation of the first noun:

wizāra*t* al-9amal   وزارة العمل وزارة العمل

Now write the same construct, but replacing *Labour* with *Economy*, *Foreign Affairs* and *Agriculture*:

wizārat al-iqtiṣād   وزارة الاقتصاد وزارة الاقتصاد
Ministry of Economy

وزارة الخارجية‬ ‫وزارة الخارجية‬ **wizārat al-khārijīya**
Ministry of Foreign Affairs

وزارة الزراعة‬ ‫وزارة الزراعة‬ **wizārat az-zirā9a**
Ministry of Agriculture

You will notice from the last two examples that the pronunciation of ة...
(if there is one) on the *last* noun does not change. It remains **-a**.

Exercise 4 Write the name of each Ministry:
(a) *Labour*   (b) *Education* (c) *Defence* (d) *Agriculture* (e) *Industry*
Read your answers aloud.

Exercise 5 Repeat Exercise 4 with *Directorate* for *Ministry*.

The answers to these exercises are given after paragraph 7 below.

3   Now ***read and write*** the following constructs:

مدير بنك‬ مدير بنك‬ **mudīr bank** *a bank manager*

موظف شركة‬ موظف شركة‬ **muwazzaf sharika**
a company employee

نمرة تلفون‬ نمرة تلفون‬ **numrat tilifōn** *a telephone number*

Do you see the difference? The last noun is now indefinite, making the
whole construct indefinite in meaning. Compare definite and indefinite
constructs with identical original elements. ***Read and write:***

مدير البنك‬ مدير البنك‬ **mudīr al-bank** *the bank manager*

مدير بنك‬ مدير بنك‬ **mudīr bank** *a bank manager*

Remember that only the last noun, i.e. the qualifier, changes, not the first
noun.

You will meet definite constructs far more often than indefinite ones.

Construct Rule 2: *A construct is definite or indefinite according to
whether the last noun is definite or indefinite.*

Exercise 6 Make indefinite constructs with these pairs of nouns. Read aloud and translate your answers:

‫(a) رئيس، وزارة (b) مدير، شركة (c) نمرة، سيّارة (d) تسجيل، عقد‬

The answers to this exercise follow paragraph 7 below.

4 So much for constructs consisting of two nouns. We also have constructs with more than two nouns. **Read and write:**

‫مكتب الضرائب والتسجيل‬
maktab aḍ-ḍarā'ib wa-t-tasjīl
Tax and Registration Office

We can call this one a *compound* construct: it has one first noun and two 'last' or qualifying nouns.

Here is another variant. **Read and write:**

‫نمرة تلفون المكتب‬ **numrat tilifōn**
al-maktab *the office telephone number*

We can call this one a *string* construct; each noun except the last one is qualified, and made definite, by the next noun.

In these two types, as in all constructs, the two construct rules given in paragraphs 2 and 3 above still apply.

5 Arabic treats the construct as a unit. An adjective is not allowed to interrupt it. Any adjective must follow the whole construct, even if confusion results. **Read and write:**

‫نمرة الشركة الجديدة‬ **numrat ash-sharika**
l-jadīda *the company's new number*
or *the new company's number*

You will meet the construct, especially the definite two-noun variety (**maktab al-mudīr**, paragraph 2 above) countless times in notices, signs, newspaper headlines and the like.

6 In Unit 3 we learned the important preposition ‫ل‬ **li** *'to, for'*. ‫ل‬ can also mean *of*, and it often allows us to make expressions which have the same meaning as a construct, but avoiding its constraints. With ل we can use the article, adjectives etc. for example, just as we wish. **Read and write** these constructs, already familiar to you:

مدير البنك   مدير البنك

نمرة الشركة   نمرة الشرك

نمرة تلفون المكتب   نمره تلغوں المكتب

نمرة الشركة الجديدة   نمره الشرك الجديره

Now see how they can all be re-expressed using ل . **Read and write:**

المدير للبنك   المديہ للبنك   al-mudīr li-l-bank

النمرة للشركة   النمره للشرك   an-numra li-sh-sharika

نمرة التلفون للمكتب* نمرة التلفوں للمكتب
                                          numrat at-tilifōn li-l-maktab

النمرة للشركة الجديدة** النمره للشرك الجديره
                                          an-numra li-sh-sharika l-jadīda

النمرة الجديدة للشركة** النمره الجديره للشرك
                                          an-numra l-jadīda li-sh-sharika

* In this example we have a construct combined with a ل expression.
** Using ل here makes it clear what is new: the company or its number.
You will see this use of ل in many advertisements, headlines and notices.

7 Descriptions, Equations and Constructs

We have studied three basic structures. It may be useful to summarise and compare their commonest forms here, to avoid confusion:

	1st Part	2nd Part	Example
Description	definite	definite	المكتب الكبير the big office
	indefinite	indefinite	مكتب كبير a big office
Equation	definite	indefinite	المكتب كبير. The office is big.
Construct	indefinite in form	definite	مكتب المدير the manager's office
		indefinite	مكتب مدير a manager's office

Exercise 7 Read out and translate these newspaper report headings:

Which expressions are constructs? Definite? Indefinite? Any 'compound' or 'string' constructs (paragraph 4 above)? What are those expressions which are not constructs?

The answers are given immediately below.

Answers to Exercises

Exercise 1 (a) **qism al-ḥisābāt** *Accounts Department*

(b) **madkhal al-wizāra** *Ministry Entrance*

(c) **mudīr al-maktab** *Office Manager*

(d) **qism at-tasjīl** *Registration Department*

(e) **istiqbāl az-zuwwār** *Visitor ('Visitors') Reception*

(f) **maktab al-madfū9āt** *Payments Office*

Exercise 2 (a) مكتب العقود **maktab al-9uqūd** *Contracts Office*

(b) قسم الهندسة **qism al-handasa** *Engineering Department*

(c) تأمين بيتي **ta'mīn baytī** *my house insurance*

(d) شغل الوزارة **shughl al-wizāra** *the ministry's work*

Exercise 3 (a) قسم المرور qism al-murūr, right

(b) مكتب الضرائب maktab aḍ-ḍarā'ib, left

(c) تسجيل السيارات tasjīl as-sayyārāt, left

(d) إصدار الرخص iṣdār ar-rukhaṣ, right

Exercise 4 (a) وزارة العمل wizārat al-9amal

(b) وزارة التربية wizārat at-tarbiya, وزارة التعليم wizārat at-ta9līm

(c) وزترة الدفاع wizārat ad-difā9

(d) وزارة الزراعة wizārat az-zirā9a

(e) وزارة الصناعة wizārat aṣ-ṣinā9a

Exercise 5 (a) دائرة العمل dā'irat al-9amal

(b) دائرة التربية dā'irat at-tarbiya, دائرة التعليم dā'irat at-ta9līm

(c) دائرة الدفاع dā'irat ad-difā9

(d) دائرة الزراعة dā'irat az-zirā9a

(e) دائرة الصناعة dā'irat aṣ-ṣinā9a

Exercise 6 (a) رئيس وزارة ra'īs wizāra *head of a ministry*

(b) مدير شركة mudīr sharika *a company manager*

(c) نمرة سيارة numrat sayyāra *a car number*

(d) تسجيل عقد tasjīl 9aqd *registration of a contract*

Exercise 7 (a) **iḍrāb al-9ummāl fī sharikat an-nafṭ** *Workers' Strike in ('the') Oil Company*, two definite constructs connected with fī

(b) **al-mashākil al-jadīda li-l-mudarā'** *Managers' New Problems*, not a construct but a definite description (Unit 9) and expression with ل

(c) **siyāsat ḥukūmat al-kuwayt** *Kuwait Government Policy*, definite 'string' construct

(d) **zuwwār al-youm** *Today's Visitors*, definite construct

(e) **si9r wa-ta'mīn al-buyūt** *Cost and Insurance of ('the') Houses*, definite compound construct

(f) **huwa l-mas'ūl**, *He is the one responsible*, not a construct but an equation with a definite second part (Unit 10).

Tests

1 Make as many meaningful constructs as possible, using a word from (a) to (e) as first noun and a word from (f) to (k) as second noun. Read each construct aloud and translate it. Is it definite or indefinite?

(c) مكتب   (b) مدير   (a) وزارة

(e) مشاكل   (d) دائرة

(h) الجمرك   (g) التجارة   (f) الشركة

(k) زميل   (j) الخارجية

2 Rewrite the word, filling in the missing letter. Read your answer aloud.

(c) ا...تظار   (b) تقر...ر   (a) ...دراء

(e) مس...ول   (d) إض..اب

3 Rewrite these constructs as expressions with ل . Read your answer aloud and translate it.

(b) سيارة زميلي المصري   (a) تأمين البيت الجديد

(d) في مكتب الجمرك   (c) مشاكل القسم الإداري

(e) شركة تأمين

4 Make these expressions plural. Read your answer aloud and translate it:

(c) مدير وموظف   (b) زائر أجنبي   (a) مشكلة كبيرة

(e) مأمور مصري   (d) عامل عربي

Review

You are now armed with a total vocabulary of just over 300 words, and three very important structures. Together, these should make intelligible much of what you see around you in signs, notices and advertisements.

You now have the knowledge to copy an unknown word or phrase accurately and later ask an Arab about it. Don't be shy about your pronunciation; listen to what you hear around you and try to imitate it, bearing in mind the brief instructions given in this book. Speak up. You learn by doing.

We now move on to the numbers, the time and the date.

13

In this unit you will learn
- numbers,
- the clock and the calendar.

New Words: * الوقت والنقود al-waqt wa-n-nuqūd *Time and Money*

1   *Essential Vocabulary*

بعد الظهر ba9d aẓ-ẓuhr *afternoon*		شهر أشهر shahr ashhur *month*	
تاريخ تواريخ tārīkh tawārīkh *date*		صباح ṣabāḥ *morning*	
جنيه jinayh *pound (£)*		صباحاً ṣabāḥan *a.m.*	
درهم دراهم dirham darāhim *dirham*		صراف ṣarrāf *money changer*	
دقيقة دقائق daqīqa daqā'iq *minute*		صرف ṣarf *exchange*	
دولار dōlār *dollar*		ظهر ẓuhr *midday*	
دينار دنانير dīnār danānīr *dinar*		مدة مدد mudda mudad *period*	
ساعة sā9a *hour*		مصرف مصارف* maṣrif maṣārif *bank*	
سنة سنوات sana sanawāt *year*		يوم أيّام youm ayyām *day*	

* In speech, use the popular words for *money*, فلوس fulūs (inanimate plural) and *bank*, بنك بنوك , the latter already known to you.

Numbers

2   Look back to Unit 7, paragraph 4, for the explanation of the Arabic numerals.

The officially correct pronunciation of the numbers, and their variable spelling as words, is complicated. Most Arabs (including educated Arabs) have difficulty with it; they prefer to use a greatly simplified colloquial pronunciation, and to avoid writing the figures in words. You are strongly advised to do the same. The colloquial pronunciation varies, but the version given below is understood and accepted by all Arabs. Beside the pronunciation you will find the variable official spellings, for recognition only. For once you are *not* being asked to 'Read and Write':

0	·	(صفر) ṣifr	1 ١	(واحد\واحدة) wāḥid(a)
2	٢			(اثنان\اثنتان\اثنين\اثنتين) ithnayn, thintayn

3 ٣ (ثلاثة\ثلاث) thalātha	4 ٤ (أربعة\أربع) arba9a
5 ٥ (خمسة\خمس) khamsa	6 ٦ (ستّة\ستّ) sitta
7 ٧ (سبعة\سبع) sab9a	8 ٨ (ثمانية\ثمان) thamāniya
9 ٩ (تسعة\تسع) tis9a	10 ١٠ (عشرة\عشر) 9ashra

We need to note:

■ wāḥid and ithnayn are masculine, wāḥida and thintayn are feminine. In counting without a noun, we use the masculine form.

■ Numbers **3** to **10** have only one spoken form. A noun following a number from **3** to **10** is made plural:

٦ عمّال (sitta) *six workmen*   ١٠ ريالات (9ashra) *ten riyals*

It may be enough for you to know the numbers up to **10**; that suffices for reading out any number. In that case, do Exercise 1 below and stop there. You can, if you wish, skim through paragraphs 3 to 7 below and treat them as reference material.

Exercise 1 In this fragment of the telephone book, find the numbers of
(a) Hassan Abu Issa   (b) Jamal Abu Issa   (c) Hamad Abu Issa

(أبو عينين...)		-٩-
٢٢٨٦٥٣	أبو عيسى جابر	٢٧٦٢٤٣	نة
٤١٩٥٦٧	أبو عيسى جمال	٤٨٩٦٤٢	في
٣٣٢٧٩٦	أبو عيسى جميل	٤٣٨٧٤١	ود
٢٣٤٣١١	أبو عيسى جميلة	٨١٩٦٥٤	ن
٦٢٦٧٩٨	أبو عيسى حسن	٦٤٥٩٠٢	لل
٥١٣٠٦٥	أبو عيسى حسني	٢٧٩٤٣٢	حي
٧١٢٦٤٠	– المكتب	٤٩٣٤٢١	
٧٣٤٨٨٥	أبو عيسى حسين	٥٧٨٠٠٨	ة
٥٣٩٨٥٤	أبو عيسى حمد	٢٣٠٩٤٥	

The answers to this exercise follow paragraph 7 below.

3 If you wish to go further with the numbers, here are first eleven to twenty, in colloquial pronunciation without the script:

11	١١	ihd9ashar	12	١٢	ithn9ashar
13	١٣	thalatt9ashar	14	١٤	arba9t9ashar
15	١٥	khamst9ashar	16	٦	sitt9ashar
17	١٧	sab9at9ashar	18	٨	thamant9ashar
19	١٩	tis9at9ashar	20	٢٠	9ishrīn

The tens from thirty to ninety:

30	٣٠	thalāthīn	40	٤٠	arba9īn
50	٥٠	khamsīn	60	٦٠	sittīn
70	٧٠	sab9īn	80	٨٠	thamānīn, thamāniyīn
90	٩٠	tis9īn			

Compounds with the tens are assembled like 'five-and-twenty' with the units first, joined to the tens with ‎و‎ *and*, pronounced colloquially **u-**. Pronounce:

21	٢١	wāhid u-9ishrīn	32	٣٢	ithnayn u-thalāthīn

From one hundred upwards, you need to recognise in script only *a hundred*, *a thousand* and *a million*:

100	١٠٠	مئة\مائة	mīya*
1000	١٠٠٠	ألف	alf
1 million	١٠٠٠٠٠٠	مليون	milyūn

Here are the duals, without the script:

200	٢٠٠	mitayn
2000	٢٠٠٠	alfayn
2 million	٢٠٠٠٠٠٠	milyūnayn

Then the other compounds, for which we use the singular of *hundred* but the plurals of *thousand* and *million*:

300-900 ٩٠٠-٣٠٠ thalāthmīya, arba9mīya, khamsmīya, sittmīya, saba9mīya, thamanmīya, tisa9mīya*

* mīya and its multiples become **mīt** before a noun:

‎موظّف‎ ١٠٠ **mīt muwazzaf** 100 employees

سنة ٥٠٠ khamsmīt sana 500 years

3000-9000   ٣٠٠٠–٩٠٠٠   thalātha, arba9a (etc.) tālāf (NB)

3-9 million   ٣٠٠٠ ٠٠٠–٩٠٠٠ ٠٠٠   thalātha (etc.) malāyīn

Read these higher compound numbers now. Note how we have **u-** *and* between the elements:

٦٤٢   sittmīya u-thnayn u-arba9īn

٣٤٨٩   thalātha tālāf u-'arba9mīya u-tis9a u-thamānīn

A noun following a number takes different forms depending on the number. Don't be confused by the different forms - you will sometimes see singulars, with or without **tanwīn** (Unit 6, paragraph 3), and sometimes plurals. There is no need to learn the rules; simply read the noun as you see it:

٥ دنانير   khamsa danānīr *five dinars*

١٥ ديناراً   khamst9ashar dīnāran *fifteen dinars*

١٥٠ دينار   mīya u-khamsīn dīnār *150 dinars*

Exercise 2 Translate:

(a) ٥٠٠ ريال   (b) ٣٦٥   (c) ٤٦ يوماً   (d) ٢٤ دولاراً   (e) ساعة دينارين

Exercise 3 Write these numbers in Arabic figures:

(a) *450*   (b) *2028*   (c) *779 4391*   (d) *404 836*   (e) *99-2440*

The answers to these exercises follow paragraph 7 below.

4   Ordinal numbers

The ordinal numbers ('first, second, third') are not difficult, and the official pronunciation is used. We need learn only 'first' to 'twelfth'. The ordinal numbers are almost always definite. *Read and write:*

the 1st   الأُولى الأوّل الاول   m. الأوّل al-'awwal, f. الأولى al-'ūla

the 2nd   الثا ني الثا نيه   m. الثاني ath-thānī, f. الثانية ath-thániya

the 3rd   الثالث الثا لثه   m. الثالث ath-thālith, f. الثالثة ath-thālitha

the 4th	الرَّابِع	الرَّابِع	ar-rābi9
the 5th	الخَامِس	الخَامِس	al-khāmis
the 6th	السَّادِس	السَّادِس	as-sādis
the 7th	السَّابِع	السَّابِع	as-sābi9
the 8th	الثَّامِن	الثَّامِن	ath-thāmin
the 9th	التَّاسِع	التَّاسِع	at-tāsi9
the 10th	العَاشِر	العَاشِر	al-9āshir
the 11th	الحَادِي عشر	الحَادِي عشر	al-ḥādī 9ashar
the 12th	الثَّانِي عشر	الثَّانِي عشر	ath-thānī 9ashar

Note the stress in the f. form **thániya** (not *thāníya*). The ordinals from *third* upwards make their feminine form in the usual way.

You will often find ordinal numbers *first* to *tenth* used in construct, instead of as an adjective. In the construct, both parts are indefinite but, strangely, the meaning is definite; and the m. form is always used, even with a f. noun. *Read and write:*

للمرَّة الثَّالثة للمرّه الثّالثه li-l-marra **th-thālitha** ⎫ *for the*
لثالث مرَّة لثالث مرّه li-**thālith** marra ⎭ *third time*

We have to write Arabic ordinals as words; there is no way of writing them with figures.

5 Fractions and percentage
We need only *half*, *third* and *quarter* from the fractions. *Read and write:*

نصف أنصاف نصف انصاف niṣf anṣāf *half*

ثلث أثلاث ثلث اثلاث thulth athlāth *third*

ربع أرباع ربع ارباع rub9 arbā9 *quarter*

ثلثين   ثلثين   thulthayn *two-thirds*

٪ ٥٠   ٪ ٥٠   khamsīn bi-l-mīya *50%*

6 Clock

One o'clock is الساعة الواحدة as-sā9a l-wāḥida. Time on the hour above *one* is written as e.g. *the ninth hour*, in definite form. *At* is في .
Read and write:

في الساعة الرابعة   فى الــا عه الرابعه   fi-s-sā9a r-rābi9a
at four o'clock

الساعة الثانية   الــا عه الثّانيه   as-sā9a th-thániya
two o'clock

Time in the first half-hour is written as follows. ***Read and write:***

الساعة الثالثة وخمس دقائق   الــا عه الثّا لثه وخمس دقائق   (wa-khamsa daqā'iq) *five past three*

الساعة السابعة والربع   الــا عه الــابعه والربع   (wa-r-rub9) *a quarter past seven*

الساعة التاسعة والثلث   الــا عه التّا ـسعه والثلث   (wa-th-thulth) *twenty past nine*

الساعة الثامنه والنصف   الــا عه الثّا منه والنصف   (wa-n-niṣf) *half-past eight*

Time in the second half-hour is written in the same way, but with إلّا illa *'except for, minus'* and the next hour. ***Read and write:***

الساعة الرابعة إلّا عشر دقائق   الــا عه الرابعه الّا عشر دقائق   (illa 9ashra daqā'iq) *ten to four*

الساعة الخامسة إلّا الربع   الــا عه الخامــه الّا الربع   (illa r-rub9) *a quarter to five*

الساعة السادسة إلّا الثلث   الــا عه الــادسه الّا الثلث   (illa th-thulth) *twenty to six*

Time written in figures is shown as follows. The style of comma may vary, and may even be replaced by the letter ر in typescript. Write:

٧,٢٠ ٧ر٣٠ *7.30*   ٤,١٥ ٤ر١٥ *4.15*   ١٠,٢٥ ١٠ر٢٥ *10.25*

7 Calendar

Read and write the days of the week:

السبت	السَّبت	as-sabt *Saturday*
الأحد	الأحد	al-'aḥad *Sunday*
الاثنين	الاثنين	al-ithnayn *Monday*
الثلاثاء	الثلاثاء	aṯ-ṯalāṯa* *Tuesday*
الأربعاء	الأربعاء	al-'arba9a* *Wednesday*
الخميس	الخميس	al-khamīs *Thursday*
الجمعه	الجمعة	al-jum9a *Friday*

* colloquial pronunciation, almost universal.

The names of the days may be preceded by يوم **youm** *day*, in construct.
On with a day is في:

في يوم السبت في يوم السبت **fī youm as-sabt** *on Saturday*

Here are the names of the months. There are two sets of names, one used
in African, the other in Asian Arab countries:

	Africa		Asia	
January	يناير	yanāyir	كانون الثاني	kānūn aṯ-ṯānī
February	فبراير	fibrāyir	شباط	shubāṭ
March	مارس	māris	آذار	ādhār
April	أبريل	abrīl	نيسان	nīsān
May	مايو	māyū	أيار	ayār
June	يونيو	yūniyū	خزيران	ḥazīrān
July	يوليو	yūliyū	تمّوز	tammūz
August	أغسطس	aghusṭus	آب	āb
September	سبتمبر	sibtambir	أيلول	aylūl

October	أكتوبر oktōbir	تشرين الأوّل	tishrīn al-awwal
November	نوفمبر nūfimbir	تشرين الثّاني	tishrīn ath-thānī
December	دسمبر disambir	كانون الأوّل	kānūn al-awwal

The Islamic calendar is also in use in some countries. The Islamic year is 354 or 355 days long. The year-count starts from the day of the flight of the prophet Muḥammad from Mecca to Medina, in 622 AD. Here are the names of the twelve months:

صفر ṣafar	٢		محرّم muḥarram	١	
ربيع الثاني rabī9 ath-thānī	٤		ربيع الأوّل rabī9 al-awwal	٣	
جمادى الآخرة jumāda l-'ākhira	٦		جمادى الأولى jumāda l-'ūla	٥	
شعبان sha9bān	٨		رجب rajab	٧	
شوّال shawwāl	١٠		رمضان ramaḍān	٩	
ذو الحجّة dhu l-ḥijja	١٢		ذو القعدة dhu l-qa9da	١١	

Dates are expressed with أوّل for the first of the month, and the ordinal numbers thereafter. Here are two typical dates, with the (colloquial) pronunciation:

١٩٨٤\٧\٢٠م   9ishrīn yūliyū/tammūz sanat alf u-tisa9mīya u-'arba9a u-thamānīn al-mīlādīya 20/7/1984 AD.

١٤١٩\٧\١هـ   awwal rajab sanat alf u-'arba9mīya u-tis9at9ashar al-hijrīya 25/7/1419 AH.

In these dates, م is ميلادية 'AD'; هـ is هجرية 'AH' which is Anno Hegiræ, the Year of the Flight.

Exercise 4 Read aloud these dates, in the Western calendar, with both Arabic forms for each month:

٢٠٠١\٨\١ (c)   ١٩٩٩\٤\٢٤ (b)   ٢٠٠٢\١٢\١٢ (a)

The answers to this exercise are on the next page.

Answers to Exercises

Exercise 1 (a) 626798 (line 5) (b) 419567 (line 2) (c) 539854 (line 9)

Exercise 2 (a) 500 riyals (b) 365 days (c) 46 dollars (d) 24 hours
(e) 2 dinars

Exercise 3 (a) ٤٥٠ (b) ٢٠٢٨ (c) ٧٧٩ ٤٣٩١ (d) ٤٠٤ ٨٣٦
(e) ٩٩-٢٤٤٠

Exercise 4 (a) ithn9ashar disambir/kānūn al-'awwal sanat alfayn u-
thnayn
(b) arba9a u-ishrīn abrīl/nīsān sanat alf u-tisa9mīya u-tis9a
u-tis9īn
(c) awwal aghustus/āb sanat alfayn u-wāḥid

Tests

1 Read aloud and translate. (The spelling of some numbers written as
words will be unfamiliar. Pronounce as shown in this unit,
irrespective of the spelling.):

(a) ستّة أسابيع   (b) خمسمئة ريال   (c) في الساعة الثامنة
(d) ١٥٪   (e) عشرين جنيهًا مصريًا
(f) في سنة ١٩٩٩   (g) جنيهين   (h) بعد الساعة ٧٠٣٠
(j) صباحًا   (k) ثلاثة آلاف ليرة

2 Read out and translate the time:

(a) ٨٠١٥   (b) الساعة الرابعة إلاّ الثلث   (c) ١٢،٢٥

Review

For the cardinal numbers, you should use the unofficial spoken form,
which is always acceptable, when reading aloud. (In fact, quoting the
numbers in official form is often regarded as somewhat precious.)

For writing the cardinal numbers, use the figures.

In the next unit we look briefly at the geography of the Arab world.

14

In this unit you will learn

■ important vocabulary for the Arab world.

New Words: العالم العربي al-9ālam al-9arabī *The Arab World*

1 It is not possible to divide this vocabulary into essential and non-essential for you; only you can do that, depending on your situation and your needs.

Vocabulary - Arab World

أبو ظبي	abū ẓabī *Abu Dhabi*	السَّعودي	as-sa9ūdīya *Saudi Arabia*
الأردن	al-'urdun *Jordan*		
الإسكندرية	al-'iskandarīya *Alexandria*	السودان	as-sūdān *Sudan*
البحرين	al-baḥrayn *Bahrain*	طرابلس	ṭarābulus *Tripoli*
بغداد	baghdād *Baghdad*	عمان	9umān *Oman*
بيروت	bayrūt *Beirut*	عمّان	9ammān *Amman*
تونس	tūnis *Tunis(ia)*	فلسطين	filasṭīn *Palestine*
الجزائر	al-jazā'ir *Algeria, Algiers*	القدس	al-quds *Jerusalem*
الخرطوم	al-khartūm *Khartoum*	قطر	qatar *Qatar*
دبي	dubayy *Dubai*	الكويت	al-kuwayt *Kuwait*
دمشق	dimashq *Damascus*	مسقط	masqaṭ *Muscat*
الدَّوحة	ad-douḥa *Doha*	المغرب	al-maghrib *Morocco*
الرباط	ar-ribāṭ *Rabat*	موريتانية	mūrītāniya *Mauritania*
الرِّياض	ar-riyāḍ *Riyadh*	اليمن	al-yaman *Yemen*

الأراضي المحتلّة al-'arāḍī l-muḥtalla *the occupied territories*

الإمارات (العربية المتّحدة) al-'imārāt (al-9arabīya l-muttaḥida) *(United Arab) Emirates*

البحر الأبيض المتوسّط al-baḥr al-'abyaḍ al-mutawassiṭ *Mediterranean Sea*

البحر الأحمر al-baḥr al-'aḥmar *the Red Sea*

الدار البيضاء ad-dār al-bayḍā' *Casablanca*

الخليج (العربي) al-khalīj (al-9arabī) *the (Arabian) Gulf*

Exercise 1 Give the Arabic names of countries (a) to (e) and cities (f) to (k) marked on the map of the Arab world following Exercise 2 below.

Exercise 2 Situate the following places on the map:

(a) البحر الأبيض المتوسّط   (b) الخليج   (c) البحر الأحمر   (d) ايران
(e) إيطاليا

بلدان ومدن عربية

The answers are given on the next page.

Answers to Exercises

Exercise 1 (a) مصر (b) السعودية (c) سوريا (d) المغرب
(e) الإمارات العربية المتّحدة (f) القاهرة (g) الخرطوم (h) مسقط
(j) بغداد (k) الجزائر

Exercise 2 This map shows the answers, and also all the Arab countries:

العالم العربي وإيطاليا وإيران

Tests

1   Make masculine singular relatives, and translate your answer:

(c) قطر   (b) عمان   (a) اليمن
                    (e) موريتانية   (d) المغرب

2   Complete the calculation in Arabic figures, and read your answer
     aloud:

$$*(b) \quad ١٨٠ : ٣ =$$ $$(a) \quad ٢٤ × ٤ =$$
$$(d) \quad ٤ + ٣ + ٢ =$$ $$(c) \quad ١٠٠ - ٨٥ =$$
$$*(: \text{is} ÷)$$ $$(e) \quad ٤٤٠ - ٥٪ =$$

Review

مبروك! Congratulations. I hope some of the mystery is now
unlocked for you. Keep practising, with every sign, notice, number,
advertisement etc. that you set your eyes on. And *write things down*.

Don't forget what is said in the Introduction about roots. You can
often untangle an unknown word by applying two tests:

■ Do *three consonants* in the word also occur, in the same order,
  in a word which you know? If so, you have a basic meaning,
  and the word is probably closely associated with it.

■ Is the *pattern* of the word familiar? Is it a participle, a verbal
  noun, an adjective? Is it a relative? An irregular plural?
  If that works, then you have scored in a further two areas:
  • you know what sort of word it is,
  • you can add the short vowels and pronounce the word.

If you get that far, you can make an informed guess at the meaning of
the new word; and, knowing its function, you can use the word
correctly in a structure.

Treat this book also as a reference manual. That is the main purpose
of the two vocabularies and the index at the back. Don't try to learn
vocabulary by heart, but rather let it come with practice.

We now move on to your final Reading Test.

15

Test Your Reading

This unit tests how well you can read now. You get no help: we are under field conditions. You can do it. Use the vocabulary only in emergency. The answers are in the key at the back of the book.

Signs
Test 1

Where are we going, and how far is it?

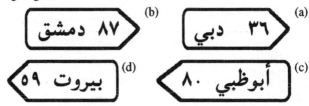

(b) ٨٧ دمشق   (a) دبي ٣٦

(d) بيروت ٥٩   (c) أبوظبي ٨٠

Test 2

What is left, what is right, and what is straight on?

Test 3

What must you do, what can't you do, and what are you requested to do?

(b) ممنوع التدخين   (a) قف وراء الخطّ

(c) ممنوع الدخول (d) الرجاء الانتظار هنا

Test 4

What part of town are we in?

(a) شارع
عبد الناصر

(b) ميدان
الاستقلال

(c) حيّ
رقم ٦

(d) شارع
القصر الجديد

Headlines
Test 5

Read the headlines aloud and translate them:

(a) شركات بريطانية في المعرض الزراعي

(b) الكل ضد تقسيم العراق ..

(c) العلاقات الاسرائيلية - الأميركية

Small print
Test 6
Look at these items and answer the questions.

(a)

This ticket was issued by a company called Najm. What sort of ticket is it? What can you do with it? What did it cost? Make a guess at '‫ل.ل.‬'. When was this ticket issued, and what is its serial number?

(b)

Who issued this banknote? What are its value and its serial number? Read aloud and translate the very small text at the top left-hand side which says:

بيروت في ٢٢ تشرين الثاني سنة ١٩٩.

Handwriting
Test 7

Match the handwritten forms (a) to (e) with the typewritten forms (f) to (k). Read them aloud:

(b) ممنون من مساعدتك   (a) تفتيش السيّارات

(d) السيّد ابو حنين   (c) في السوق

(e) من بيروت الى عمّان

(f) السيّد أبو حسنين

(g) في السوق

(h) من بيروت الى عمّان

(j) تفتيش السيّارات

(k) ممنون من مساعدتك

Test 8

Read this handwritten note aloud and translate it:

السيّد بُراونه" : السّائق ابوبكر حاضر في السّاعه السّابعه والنصف صباحًا لزيارة الجيزه .

Using a directory
Test 9

Put these directory entries into alphabetical order:

وزارة المالية، أبوبكر، بلدية، مجلس الثقافة، شلّ لبنان، مدرسة ثانوية، سفارة تونس، غرفة التجارة، نجم، المكتبة الحديثة.

Test 10

Under what Arabic word would you first look for the following in a telephone book?

(a) Nimr Bus Company   (b) Kuwaiti Embassy   (c) Munir Rais & Sons

(d) Habib's Insurance   (e) El-Nur Moroccan Restaurant

If that didn't work, under what word would you make your second attempt? And any further attempts?

What next?

You may want to take your new knowledge of Arabic further, and learn to read and write continuous text. This is certainly possible.

If you want to learn spoken Arabic, then bear in mind that there are differences between the written and spoken languages. Spoken Arabic is easier than written, and is best learned in transcription, since there is no official way of writing it anyway.

Here are a few suggestions for extending your study of Arabic.

Coursebooks and audio materials for self-tuition

Written Arabic:

- ■ *Teach Yourself Arabic*, J. Smart, Hodder & Stoughton, book ISBN 0340 772727, book + cassettes 0340 727735, book + CDs 0340 802812 .

Spoken and written Arabic:

- ■ *Arabic Today*, J. Mace, Edinburgh University Press, book ISBN 0748 606165, cassette available from Edinburgh University Press, tel. +44 (0)131 650 8436, fax +44 (0)131 662 9953.

Spoken Arabic:

- ■ *Teach Yourself Gulf Arabic*, J. Smart & F. Altorfer, Hodder & Stoughton, book ISBN 0340 721251, book + cassettes 0340 747471.

- ■ *Eastern Arabic*, F. Rice & M. Said, Georgetown University Press, book ISBN 0878 400214; cassettes available separately.

Dictionaries See page 53.

Websites offering on-line courses

- ■ *www.i-cias.com*. From Cairo, spoken and written Arabic.
- ■ *www.arabic2000.com*. Several courses.

Short residential courses in the Middle East and North Africa

- ■ *www.languagesabroad.com*.
- ■ *www.studyabroad.com*.

Arabic script software

- ■ *www.babel.uoregon.edu./yamada/fonts/arabic.htm*.

  A long list. Be sure to select software which provides not only the alphabet but also the essential right-to-left writing direction. (NB: This book is set in the classic Arabic font called *Baghdad*.)

KEY to TESTS

Unit 1

1 (b) بيتين (c) ابني (d) اثاثي (e) نبات

2 (b) baytáyn (c) íbnī (d) aṯháṯī (e) nabát

3 (b) iṯnáyn (c) yābánī (d) áyna (e) íbnī

4 (b) بنتين (c) بناياتي (d) بابين (e)اين (f) اثاثي

5 (b) bāb; middle alif (c) āb; alif madda (d) nabát; middle alif
(e) iṯnáyn; alif at the beginning shows a short vowel (here, i)

Unit 2

1 (b)التمويل (c)اوّل (d) الماني (e) ممنون

2 (b) at-tamwíl (c) áwwal (d) almánī (e) mamnún

3 (b) áwwal (c) aṯ-ṯálith (d) mamnún (e) an-naml

4 (b) ممثّلين (c)التّمويل (d) النّيلين (e) او (f) اليابني

5

	nationalities
الماني، ياباني، لبناني، ليبي	nationalities
الثالث، اوّل، اثنين، ثلاث	numbers
يونيو، يوليو، آب، مايو	months
البيوت، البنايات	buildings

Unit 3

1 (b) الاسم (c)الممثّل (d) أنباء (e) ثنائي

2 (b) al-ism (c) al-mumáṯṯhil (d) anbá’ (e) ṯhuná’ī

3 (b) al-lubnāníya (c) al-’almāníya (d) bi-l-’áwwal
(e) bi-ṯ-ṯálitha

4 (b) ياباني (c) اللبناني (d) مسؤول (e) للثالث

5 (b) yābánī (c) al-lubnánī (d) mas’úl (e) li-ṯ-ṯálith

6 (b) اهتمام (c)الملابس (d) البيوت (e) ثانوي

Unit 4

1 (a) مصريه (b) ١ هتمام (c) تمام (d) ضروري (e) الماني

2 (a) miṣrîya (b) ihtimâm (c) tamâm (d) ḍarûrī (e) almânī

3 (a) al-'īrānîya (b) marîḍ (c) li-s-sūrîya (d) ibtidâ'ī
(e) bi-l-'almânīya

4 (a) أساس basis, أساسي basic (b) دراسة study, دراسي academic
(c) إدارة administration, إداري administrative
(d) ليبيا Libya, لليبية for the Libyan (woman)
(e) إسرائيل Israel, الإسرائيلية the Israeli (woman)

5 (a) asâs (b) dirása (c) idára (d) lîbiya (e) isrâ'īl

6 (a) المصرية (b) إدارة (c) مدير (d) الشّيء (e) مريضة

Unit 5

1 (a) ash-shay' the thing (b) mas'ūla responsible
(c) as-si9r the price (d) madkhal entrance
(e) al-intikhāb the election

2 (b) السّنة (d) الشّهر (c) الأسبوع (a) اليوم

3 (a) صناعي industrial (b) ابتدائي initial, primary
(c) أسبوعي weekly (d) إيطالي Italian (e) بريطاني British

4 (a) التأسيس (b) النهائي (c) مسؤول (d) المخرج (e) الدخول

Unit 6

1 (a) ṣinā9a industry (b) maṭār airport (c) mas'ūl responsible
(d) wizāra ministry (e) idāra administration (f) akhbār news
(g) iḥtijāj objection (h) sharika company (j) ow or (k) sūq market
(m) mathalan for example (n) mustashfa hospital

2 (a) معلم mu9allim (b) مكتب maktab (c) فوراً fouran
(d) تأسيس ta'sīs (e) ابتدائي ibtidā'ī

3 (a) Kodak (b) IBM (c) Mobil (d) Michelin (e) Peugeot

Unit 7

1   (a) **al-9irāq** *Iraq* (b) **al-qāhira** *Cairo* (c) **sharika** *company*
(d) **mumkin** *possible* (e) **ziyāra** *visit* (f) **idārī** *administrative*
(g) **mumaththilīn** *representatives* (h) **as-sūrīyīn** *the Syrians*
(j) **maḥkama** *law-court* (k) **ajnabī** *foreign* (m) **madāris** *schools*
(n) **al-intikhābāt** *the elections*

2

مدارس، مشاكل، مطاعم، عواصم، مبالغ، محاكم

أسابيع، أساليب

بيوت، خطوط، ظروف، بنوك

أخبار، أرقام، أموال، أفكار

مدراء، وزراء، وكلاء

3   (a) سوريين (b) إيرانيين (c) مصريين (d) عراقيين (e) كويتيين

4   (a) البنايات (b) السّفارات (c) مستشفيات (d) كمبيوترات
(e) إوتيلات (f) معلّمات (g) المطارات (h) منظّمات
(j) شركات (k) إمكانيات (m) الزّيارات (n) انتخابات

Unit 8

1   (a) **taqdīm** verbal noun (b) **rākib** active participle
(c) **murāsil** active participle (d) **indhār** verbal noun
(e) **musta9lim** active participle (f) **shāmil** active participle
(g) **iftitāḥ** verbal noun (h) **sāmi9** active participle
(j) **mudarris** active participle (k) **istithmār** verbal noun

2   (a) مناسبة (b) انتخابي (c) مقرّرين (d) عمّال (e) تنظيم

3   (a) مفتّش **mufattish** *inspector,* تفتيش **taftīsh** *inspection*
(b) مشترك **mushtarik** *joint, common,* اشتراك **ishtirāk**
participation
(c) مرسل **mursil** *sender,* إرسال **irsāl** *despatch*
(d) مساعد **musā9id** *assistant,* مساعدة **musā9ada** *help*
(e) مستقبل **mustaqbil** *receiver,* استقبال **istiqbāl** *reception*

4   (a) **al-istiqbāl** (b) **madrasa li-l-banāt** (c) **miṣr wa-l-9irāq**
(d) **īrān** (e) **al-qāhira**

Unit 9

1   (a) **ṣiḥāfatna l-'usbū9īya** *our weekly press*

(b) **iḥtijājāthum aṭ-ṭawīla** *their long objections*

(c) **az-zumalā' al-fannīyīn** *the technical colleagues*

(d) **ṣuḥuf 9arabīya** *Arab(ic) newspapers*

(e) **bank ajnabī** *a foreign bank*

2   (a) مدرسة ابتدائية   (b) المطار الوطني   (c) تقاريره اليومية
(d) لزوّارنا الأجانب   (e) انتخابات عامّة

3   (a) رسالات طويلة   (b) التقارير الفنّية   (c) ممثّلين أجانب
(d) الطائرات الأميركية   (e) خطوط جوّية

Unit 10

1   (a) **waẓīfatu ṣa9ba.** *His job is difficult.*

(b) **al-mu'tamar at-tijārī hāmm.**
The trade conference is important.

(c) **al-wuzarā' moujūdūn.** *The ministers are present.*

(d) **aṣ-ṣūra jamīla.** *The picture/photograph is beautiful.*

(e) **aṣ-ṣūra l-jamīla** *the beautiful picture/photograph*

2   (a) الموظّفون مسرورون. **al-muwaẓẓafūn masrūrūn**
The employees are pleased.

(b) مطارنا الدولي هامّ. **maṭārna d-duwalī hāmm.**
Our international airport is important.

(c) هو تاجر دولي. **huwa tājir duwalī.**
He is an international trader.

(d) النصّ واضح ومقبول. **an-naṣṣ wāḍiḥ wa-maqbūl.**
The text is clear and acceptable.

(e) المأمور مشغول. **al-ma'mūr mashghūl.** *The official is busy.*

3   (a) وظيفة **waẓīfa** *job*   (b) موظّف **muwaẓẓaf** *employee*

(c) مندوب **mandūb** *delegate*   (d) غائب **ghā'ib** *absent*

(e) الخبراء **al-khubarā'** *the experts*

Unit 11

1   (a) **mamnū9 al-intiẓār** *WAITING PROHIBITED*
(b) **fi l-balad** *in (the) town*
(c) **fi l-bilād** *in the towns/in the country*
(d) **ashghāl 9ala ṭ-ṭarīq** *road works ('works on the road')*
(e) **al-murūr ila l-yamīn** *turning right*

2   (a) سيّارات جديدة   (b) أشغال هامّة   (c) الشُّرطة المحلّية
(d) مستشفيات كبيرة   (e) مشاكل فنّية

3   (a) **al-ma'mūr al-mas'ūl** *the responsible official*; Description
(b) **al-ma'mūrūn hum al-mas'ūlūn** *The officials are those*
   responsible ('the responsible ones'). Equation
(c) **al-bilād jamīl** *The country is beautiful*. Equation
(d) **zamīlī fi l-mustashfa** *My colleague is in hospital*. Equation
(e) **zamīlī l-marīḍ** *my sick colleague*; Description

Unit 12

1   (a) + (g) وزارة التجارة **wizārat at-tijāra**
   Ministry of Trade, definite
(a) + (j) وزارة الخارجية **wizārat al-khārijīya**
   Ministry of Foreign Affairs, definite
(b) + (f) مدير الشركة **mudīr ash-sharika**
   The company director, definite
(b) + (g) مدير التجارة **mudīr at-tijāra** *Director of Trade*, definite
(b) + (h) مدير الجمرك **mudīr al-jumruk**
   Director of Customs, definite
(b) + (j) مدير الخرجية **mudīr al-khārijīya**
   Director of Foreign Affairs, definite
(c) + (f) مكتب الشركة **maktab ash-sharika**
   the company office, definite
(c) + (g) مكتب التجارة **maktab at-tijāra** *Trade Office*, definite
(c) + (h) مكتب الجمرك **maktab al-jumruk**
   Customs Office, definite

(c) + (j) مكتب الخارجية maktab al-<u>kh</u>ārijīya
Office of Foreign Affairs, definite

(c) + (k) مكتب زميل maktab zamīl
a colleague's office, indefinite

(d) + (g) دائرة التجارة dā'irat at-tijāra
Directorate of Trade, definite

(d) + (h) دائرة الجمرك dā'irat al-jumruk
Customs Directorate, definite

(d) + (j) دائرة الخارجية dā'irat al-<u>kh</u>ārijīya
Directorate of Foreign Affairs, definite

(e) + (f) مشاكل الشركة ma<u>sh</u>ākil a<u>sh</u>-<u>sh</u>arika
the company's problems, definite

(e) + (g) مشاكل التجارة ma<u>sh</u>ākil at-tijāra
the problems of trade, definite

(e) + (h) مشاكل الجمرك ma<u>sh</u>ākil al-jumruk
(the) Customs problems, definite

(e) + (j) مشاكل الخارجية ma<u>sh</u>ākil al-<u>kh</u>ārijīya
(the) Foreign Affairs problems, definite

(e) + (k) مشاكل زميل ma<u>sh</u>ākil zamīl
a colleague's problems, indefinite

2   (a) مدراء mudarā'   (b) تقرير taqrīr   (c) انتظار inti<u>z</u>ār
     (d) إضراب i<u>d</u>rāb   (e) مسؤول mas'ūl

3   (a) التأمين للبيت الجديد at-ta'mīn li-l-bayt al-jadīd
     the insurance of the new house

     (b) السيارة لزميلي المصري as-sayyāra li-zamīlī l-mi<u>s</u>rī
     my Egyptian colleague's car

     (c) المشاكل للقسم الإداري al-ma<u>sh</u>ākil li-l-qism al-'idārī
     Administration Department's problems

     (d) في المكتب للجمرك fi l-maktab li-l-jumruk
     in the Customs Office

     (e) شركة للتأمين <u>sh</u>arika li-t-ta'mīn *an insurance company*

4 (a) مشاكل كبيرة mashākil kabīra *big problems*

(b) زوّار أجانب zuwwār ajānib *foreign visitors*

(c) مدراء وموظّفين\...ون mudarā' wa-muwaẓẓafīn/muwaẓẓafūn *directors and employees*

(d) عمّال عرب 9ummāl 9arab *Arab workers*

(e) مأمورين مصريين\مأمورون مصريون ma'mūrīn miṣrīyīn/ ma'mūrūn miṣrīyūn *Egyptian officials*

Unit 13

1 (a) sitt(a) asābī9 *six weeks*

(b) **khamsmīt** riyāl *five hundred riyals*

(c) fi s-sā9a **th-thāmina** *at eight o'clock*

(d) **khamst9ashar** bi-l-mīya *fifteen per cent*

(e) 9ishrīn jinayhan miṣrīyan *twenty Egyptian pounds*

(f) fī sanat alf u-tisa9mīya u-tis9a u-tis9īn *in 1999*

(g) jinayhayn *two pounds*

(h) ba9d as-sā9a s-sābi9a wa n-niṣf *after seven-thirty*

(j) ṣabāḥan *a.m./in the morning*

(k) **thalātha** tālāf līra *three thousand lira*

2 (a) as-sā9a **th-thāmina** wa-r-rub9 *a quarter past eight*

(b) as-sā9a r-rābi9a illa **th-thulth** *twenty to four*

(c) as-sā9a **th-thāniya** 9ashara wa-**khamsa** u-9ishrīn *twenty-five past twelve*

Unit 14

1 (a) اليمني *(the) Yemeni* (b) عماني *Omani* (c) قطري *Qatari*

(d) المغربي *(the) Moroccan* (e) موريتاني *Mauritanian*

2 (a) ٩٦ = ٤ × ٢٤ sitta u-tis9īn

(b) ٦٠ = ٣ : ١٨٠ sittīn

(c) ٧٠ = ٨٥ − ١٥٥ sab9īn

(d) ٩ = ٢ + ٣ + ٤ tis9a

(e) £٣٨ = ٪٥ − £٤٠ **thamāniya** u-**thalāthīn** jinayh

Unit 15

1 (a) *Dubai 36* (b) *Damascus 87* (c) *Abu Dhabi 80* (d) *Beirut 59*

2 Left: *Market, Ministries, Parliament*   Right: *Airport*
Straight on: *National University, Technical Schools, Girls'
Secondary School*

3 (a) *Stop behind the Line* (b) *No Smoking* (c) *No Entry*
(d) *Please Wait Here*

4 (a) *Abdel Nasser* (**9abd an-nāsir**) *Street* (b) *Independence Square*
(c) *District no. 6* (d) *New Palace Street*

5 (a) s̲h̲arikāt barīṭānīya fi l-ma9riḍ az-zirā9ī *British Companies
in Agricultural Exhibition*

(b) **al-kull ḍidd taqsīm al-9irāq** *All are against the partition of
Iraq*

(c) **al-9alāqāt al-'isrā'īlīya-al-'amayrkīya** *Israeli-American
Relations*

6 (a) A bus ticket from Tripoli (Lebanon) to Beirut. The fare is 3500
Lebanese lira (ل.ل), the date 5/6/1999 and the serial number 8456.
(b) Note issued by the Bank of Lebanon, value 1000 lira, serial
number 9205319 $\frac{T3}{7}$. The text reads: **bayrūt fī t̲h̲nayn u-9is̲h̲rīn
tis̲h̲rīn at̲h̲-t̲h̲ānī sanat alf u-tisa9mīya u-tis9īn.** *Beirut, 22
November* 1990.

7 (a) and (j) **taftīs̲h̲ as-sayyārāt**
(b) and (k) **mamnūn min musā9adatak**
(c) and (g) **fi s-sūq**
(d) and (f) **as-sayyid abū ḥasanayn**
(e) and (h) **min bayrūt ila 9ammān**

8 **as-sayyid Brown: as-sāi'q abū bakr ḥāḍir fi s-sā9a s-sābi9a
wa-n-niṣf ṣabāḥan li-ziyārat al-gīza.** *Mr Brown: Driver Abu Bakr
ready at 7.30 a.m. for the visit to ('of') Giza.*

9
أبو بكر، بلدية، سفارة تونس، شلّ لبنان، غرفة التجارة،
مجلس الثقافة، مدرسة ثانوية، المكتبة الحديثة، نجم،
وزارة المالية

10 Search in the order shown:
(a) نمر، شركة، أوتوبيس، باص، نقل (b) سفارة، كويت
(c) رئيس، منير، شركة (d) تأمين، حبيب، شركة (e) مطعم، نور

VOCABULARIES

In both these vocabularies:

- ■ Entries are referred by number to the page with the first and other important appearances of the Arabic word.
- ■ Arabic irregular plurals are listed with the singular. Where no plural is shown, it is regular.
- ■ The command form of the verb (pages 94 and 95) is shown with '*!*' after the English, for clarity.

Arabic-English Vocabulary

For this vocabulary, you can find the alphabetical order of the Arabic letters and non-alphabetical signs on pages 52 and 53. Further, in this vocabulary:

- ■ Arabic irregular plurals are also listed separately with a reference (marked '→') to the singular.
- ■ Words used only or mainly with the article ...ال are listed with the article, but in the alphabetical position of the word itself.

آ ا أ إ آ

أب آباء **ab ābā'** *father* 7

أب **āb** *August* 7, 115

أب → آباء

ابتداء **ibtidā'** *beginning* 34

ابتدائي **ibtidā'ī** *initial, primary* 37

أبريل **abrīl** *April* 115

إبل **ibil** *camels* 14

ابن ابناء **ibn abnā'** *son* 8

ابن → ابناء

أبو ظبي **abū ẓabī** *Abu Dhabi* 118

باب → أبواب

بحر → أبيض

أثاث **athāth** *furniture* 7

ثلث → أثلاث

اثنين **ithnayn** *two* 10, 109; الاثنين **al-ithnayn** *Monday* 115

أجنبي → أجانب

اجتماع **ijtimā9** *meeting* 44, 71

أجر أجور ajr ujūr *wage* 84

أجنبي أجانب ajnabī ajānib

foreign 41, 73

أجر → أجور

احتجاج iḥtijāj *objection* 41

الأحد al-'aḥad *Sunday* 115

بحر → أحمر

خبر → أخبار

خطر → أخطار

خطاب → أخطبة

إدارة idāra *admin-*

istration 34, 70

آذار ādhār *March* 115

الأراضي المحتلة al-'arāḍī

l-muḥtalla *the occupied*

territories 118

ربع → أرباع

الأربعاء al-'arba9a

Wednesday 115

أربعة arba9a *four* 110

إرسال irsāl *despatch* 70

الأردن al-'urdun

Jordan 118

رقم → أرقام

اركب irkab *get on!* 94

أسبوع → أسابيع

أستاذ → أساتذة

أساس أسس asās usus *basis* 29

أساسي asāsī *basic* 37

أسبوع أسابيع usbū9 asābī9

week 44, 60

أستاذ أساتذة ustādh asātidha

professor 34

استثمار istithmār

investment 50

استخدام istikhdām *employ-*

ment, recruitment 70

استعمال isti9māl *use* 50

استقبال istiqbāl

reception 50, 70

استقلال istiqlāl

independence 50, 71

استكشاف istikshāf

exploration 50

استنكار istinkār *rejection* 50

إسرائيل isrā'īl *Israel* 61

إسرائيلي isrā'īlī *Israeli* 37

أسس → أساس

سعر → أسعار

الإسكندرية al-'iskandarīya

Alexandria 118

اسكوتلندا iskotlanda

Scotland 54

اسم أسماء ism asmā' *name* 29

اسم → أسماء

سوق → أسواق

سؤال → أسئلة

إشارة ishāra *sign* 91

اشرب ishrab *drink!* 94

اشتراك ishtirāk

participation 70

اشتراكي ishtirākī
socialist 70

اشتراكية ishtirākīya
socialism 70

أشغال → شغل

أشكال → شكل

أشهر → شهر

أشياء → شيء

إصدار iṣdār issue 73

إصلاح iṣlāḥ reform 71

أصوات → صوت

إضراب iḍrāb strike 35, 70

أطبّاء → طبيب

اطلب uṭlub ask for...! 94

إعلان i9lān announce-
ment, notice,
advertisement 73

أعمال → عمل

أغسطس aghusṭus
August 115

افتح iftaḥ open! 94

أفلام → فلم

اقتراح iqtirāḥ
proposal 50, 55

اقتصاد iqtiṣād economy,
economics 99

أقسام → قسم

اقفل iqfil shut! 94

أقلّاء → قليل

أكتوبر oktōbir
October 116

أكثر akthar more 50, 55

آلات ālāt tools 15

ألف alf thousand 111

الآن al-'ān now 24

ألله allāh God 27

ألماني almānī German 16

ألمانيا almāniya
Germany 36

ألوان → لون

إلي ila to 52, 91

الإمارات (العربية المتّحدة)
al-'imārāt (al-9arabīya
l-muttaḥida) (United
Arab) Emirates 118

أمام amām
in front of 15, 91

أمتار → متر

إمكانية imkānīya
possibility 50

أميركا amayrka America 61

أميركي → أميركان
أميركي أميركان\أميركيون\
...يين   amayrkī amayrkān/
amayrkīyūn/-īyīn
American 61

أنا ana I 9, 85

أنباء → نبأ

أنت anta, anti you 9, 85

إنتاج intāj production 41

انتباه intibāh caution 27

انتخاب intikhāb
election 41, 70

انتظار intizār
wait(ing) 70, 95

انتقال intiqāl transfer 71

أنتم antum you 16, 85

إنجليزي → إنجليز

إنجليزي إنجليز ingilīzī ingilīz
English, British 60

انزل inzil get off! 94

أنصاف → نصف

انظر unzur see...! 94

اهتمام ihtimām
attention 27

أو ow or 18

أوتوبيس otobīs bus 54

أوتيل ōtēl hotel 54

أوطان → وطن

أوقات → وقت

أول awwal first 18, 112

أولى ūla first 112

أيّام → يوم

إيران īrān Iran 33

إيراني īrānī Iranian 36

إيطالي īṭālī Italian 58

إيطاليا īṭāliya Italy 42

إيقاف īqāf parking 91

أيار ayār May 115

أيلول aylūl
September 115

أين ayna where 11

ب

ب bi- with, by, in 25, 91

باب أبواب bāb abwāb door 7

باريس pārīs Paris 54

باص bāṣ bus 35

باكستان pākistān Pakistan 61

البحر الأبيض المتوسّط al-baḥr
al-'abyaḍ al-mutawassiṭ
Mediterranean Sea 118

البحر الأحمر al-baḥr al-'aḥmar
Red Sea 118

البحرين al-baḥrayn
Bahrain 118

بدون bidūn without 91

برلمان barlamān
parliament 92

بريد barīd mail 73

بريطانيا barīṭāniya Britain 42

بطالة baṭāla
unemployment 84

بعد ba9d after 91; بعد
بعد الظهر ba9d aẓ-ẓuhr
afternoon, p.m. 109

بغداد baghdād
Baghdad 118

بلاد → بلد

بلاد بلدان bilād buldān
country 73

بلد بلاد balad bilād
town 91

بلاد → بلدان

بلدية baladīya
town hall 92

بنت → بنات

بنت بنات bint banāt
girl, daughter 8

بنك بنوك bank bunūk
bank 49, 60

بنك → بنوك

بوليس būlīs *police* 91

بيت بيوت bayt buyūt
house 9, 60

بيروت bayrūt *Beirut* 118

دار → بيضاء

بيت → بيوت

ت

تاجر تجّار tājir tujjār
trader 84

تاريخ تواريخ tārīkh tawārīkh
date 109

تاسع tāsi9 *ninth* 113

تأسيس ta'sīs
foundation 29

تأمين ta'mīn
insurance 99

تاجر → تجّار

تجارة tijāra *trade* 73

تجديد tajdīd *renewal* 71

تحت taht *below, under* 91

تحسين tahsīn *repair* 50

تدخين tadkhīn *smoking* 91

تدريس tadrīs *instruction* 71

تربية tarbiya *education* 99

تسجيل tasjīl *registration* 99

تسعة tis9a *nine* 110

تشرين الأوّل tishrīn al-'awwal
October 116

تشرين الثاني tishrīn ath-thānī
November 116

تعليم ta9līm *tuition,
education* 50, 69

تعليمي ta9līmī *educational,
tutorial* 70

تفتيش taftīsh
inspection 48, 69

تقديم taqdīm
presentation 73

تقرير → تقارير

تقرير taqrīr
decision 49, 61, 69

تقرير تقارير taqrīr taqārīr
report 49, 61, 69

تقسيم taqsīm *partition* 50

تكليف → تكاليف

تكليف تكاليف taklīf takālīf
cost 50

تلّ تلال tall tilāl *hill* 19

تلّ → تلال

تلفون tilifōn *telephone* 54

تليفزيون tilivizyūn *television* 73

تليفون tilīfōn *telephone* 54

تمام tamām *perfect* 16

تمهّل tamahhal *slow down!* 27, 94

تمّوز tammūz *July* 115

تمويل tamwīl *financing* 17, 71

تنبّؤ tanabbu' *forecast* 24

تنبيه tanbīh *warning* 27

تنظيم tanẓīm *organisation* 42, 69

تاريخ → تواريخ

توقيف touqīf *parking* 91

تونس tūnis *Tunis(ia)* 118

ث

ثابت thābit *firm, solid* 7

ثالث thālith *third* 14, 112

ثامن thāmin *eighth* 113

ثانوي thānawī *secondary* 17

ثاني thānī *second* 112

ثاني عشر thānī 9ashar *twelfth* 113

ثلاث\ثلاثة thalāth(a) *three* 15, 110

الثلاثاء ath-thalātha *Tuesday* 115

ثلث أثلاث thulth athlāth *a third* 113

ثمانية thamāniya *eight* 110

ثنائي thunā'ī *double* 24

ج

چاكارتا jakārta *Jakarta* 54

جامعة jāmi9a *university* 92

جديد → جدد

جديد جدد jadīd judud *new* 73

جريدة → جرائد

جراچ garāj *garage* 91

جريدة جرائد jarīda jarā'id *newspaper* 74

الجزائر al-jazā'ir *Algeria, Algiers* 118

جمادى الآخرة jumāda l-'ākhira *see* 116

جمادى الأولى jumāda l-'ūla *see* 116

جمرك jumruk *customs* 99

الجمعة al-jum9a *Friday* 115

جميل jamīl *beautiful* 73

جنوب janūb *south* 41

جنوبي janūbī *southern* 41

جنيف jinēv *Geneva* 54

جنيه jinayh *pound (£)* 109

جوّي jawwī
air (adjective) 73

ح

حادى عشر ḥādī 9ashar
eleventh 113

حاضر ḥāḍir
present, ready 67

حدّ حدود ḥadd ḥudūd
limit 91

حديث → حداث

حدّ → حدود

حديث حداث ḥadīth ḥidāth
modern 73

حزيران ḥazīrān June 115

حساب ḥisāb account 99

حسب ḥasab
according to 91

حكومة ḥukūma
government 73

خ

خارج khārij outside 91

خارجية khārijīya
Foreign Affairs 99

خاصّ khāṣṣ private,
special, particular 41

خاصّةً khāṣṣatan
specially 51

خامس khāmis fifth 113

خبر أخبار khabar akhbār
news item 41, 59

خبير → خبراء

خبير خبراء khabīr khubarā'
expert 84

الخرطوم al-khartūm
Khartoum 118

خروج khurūj exit 41

خطّ خطوط khaṭṭ khuṭūṭ
line 42, 60

خطاب أخطبة khiṭāb akhṭiba
speech 73

خطر أخطار khaṭar akhṭār
danger 42, 59

خطر khaṭir dangerous 42

خطّ → خطوط

خلال khilāl during 91

الخليج (العربي) al-khalīj
(al-9arabī)
(Arabian) Gulf 118

خمسة khamsa five 110

الخميس al-khamīs
Thursday 115

خياطة khiyāṭa sewing 62

د

داخل dākhil inside 91

داخلية dākhilīya
Home Affairs 99

الدار البيضاء ad-dār al-bayḍā'
Casablanca 118

دائرة دوائر dā'ira dawā'ir
directorate 34, 99

دبيّ dubayy Dubai 118

دخول dukhūl entry 41

دراسة dirāsa study 34

دراسي dirāsī academic 37

درهم → دراهم

درهم دراهم dirham darāhim
dirham 109

دسمبر disambir
December 116

دفاع difā9 defence 99

دفع مدفوعات daf9 madfū9āt
payment 99

دقيقة → دقائق

دقيقة دقائق daqīqa daqā'iq
minute 109

دمشق dimashq
Damascus 118

دموقراطية dimuqrātīya
democracy 70

دينار → دنانير

دائرة → دوائر

الدّوحة ad-douha
Doha 118

دولار dōlār dollar 109

دولي duwalī
international 84

دون dūn without 91

دينار دنانير dīnār danānīr
dinar 109

ذ

ذو الحجّة dhu l-ḥijja see 116

ذو القعدة dhu l-qa9da
see 116

ر

رابع rābi9 fourth 113

راتب رواتب rātib rawātib
salary 84

راديو rādiō radio 73

الرّباط ar-ribāṭ Rabat 118

ربع أرباع rub9 arbā9
a quarter 113

ربيع الأوّل rabī9 al-'awwal
see 116

ربيع الثّاني rabī9 ath-thānī
see 116

الرجاء ar-rajā' please... 95

رجب rajab see 116

رخصة → رخص

رخصة رخص rukhsa rukhas
licence 99

رسالة risāla letter 73

رسمي rasmī official 73

رسميّاً rasmīyan
officially 51

رقم أرقام raqm arqām
number 49

رمضان ramaḍān see 116

راتب → رواتب

سباكة sibāka

plumbing 62

السَّبت as-sabt

Saturday 115

سبتمبر sibtambir

September 115

سبعة sab9a seven 110

ستة sitta six 110

سرعة sur9a speed 91

سعر أسعار si9r as9ār

price 44, 59

سفير ← سفراء

سفارة sifāra embassy 48

سفير سفراء safīr sufarā'

ambassador 48

ساكن ← سكّان

سلام salām peace 93

سمسار ← سماسير

سمسار سماسير simsār samāsīr

broker 84

سنة سنوات sana sanawāt

year 29, 109

سنة ← سنوات

السَّعودية as-sa9ūdīya

Saudi Arabia 118

السّودان as-sūdān Sudan 118

سؤال أسئلة su'āl as'ila

question 29

سوري sūrī Syrian 36

سوريا sūriya Syria 36

رئيس ← رؤساء

روما rōma Rome 54

الرّياض ar-riyāḍ

Riyadh 118

ريال riyāl rial, riyal 33

رئيس رؤساء ra'īs ru'asā'

chairman, chief,

president, head 33

رئيسي ra'īsī

main, principal 37

ز

زائر زوّار zā'ir zuwwār

visitor 62

زراعة zirā9a

agriculture 99

زميل ← زملاء

زميل زملاء zamīl zumalā'

colleague 73

زائر ← زوّار

زيارة ziyāra visit 33

س

سابع sābi9 seventh 113

سادس sādis sixth 113

سيّد ← سادة

ساعة sā9a hour 109

ساكن سكّان sākin sukkān

resident 50

سائق sā'iq

driver 50, 67, 68

سوق أسواق sūq aswāq (f.)
market 49

سويسرا swisira
Switzerland 54

سياحة siyāḥa *tourism* 62

سيّارة sayyāra *car* 33

سياسة siyāsa
policy, politics 99

سيّد سادة sayyid sāda
Mr, gentleman 34

سيّدة sayyida
Mrs, lady 34

ش

شارع shāri9 shawāri9
street 44

شاي shāy *tea* 29

شباط shubāṭ
February 115

شخصي shakhṣī
personal 73

شرطة shurṭa *police* 42

شرطي shurṭī
policeman 92

شرق sharq *east* 49

شركة sharika
company 49

شعبان sha9bān see 116

شغل أشغال shughl ashghāl
work, job 84

شكل أشكال shakl ashkāl
form 50, 55

شمال shimāl *north* 29

شمالي shimālī
northern 29

شمس shams *sun* 29

شهر أشهر shahr ashhur
month 33, 109

شارع → شوارع

شوّال shawwāl see 116

شيء أشياء shay' ashyā'
thing 29, 59

ص

صباح ṣabāḥ *morning* 109

صباحًا ṣabāḥan *a.m.* 109

صحافة ṣiḥāfa *press* 73

صحيفة → صحف

صحفي ṣuḥufī *journalist* 73

صحيفة صحف ṣaḥīfa ṣuḥuf
newspaper 73

صرّاف ṣarrāf
money changer 109

صرف ṣarf *exchange* 109

صعب → صعاب

صعب صعاب ṣa9b ṣi9āb
difficult 84

صغير → صغار

صغير صغار ṣaghīr ṣighār
small 50

صفر ṣifr *zero* 109;
ṣafar *see* 116

صناعة ṣinā9a *industry* 44

صوت أصوات ṣowt aṣwāt
voice 35

صورة → صور

صورة صور ṣūra ṣuwar *picture,
photograph* 73

ض

ضدّ ḍidd *against* 91

ضريبة → ضرائب

ضرورة ḍarūra
necessity 35

ضروري ḍarūrī
necessary 36

ضريبة ضرائب ḍarība ḍarā'ib
tax 99

ط

طالب طلاب ṭālib ṭullāb
student 68

طائرة ṭā'ira *aeroplane* 42

طبيب أطبّاء ṭabīb aṭibbā'
doctor 84

طرابلس ṭarābulus
Tripoli 118

طريق → طرق

طريق طرق ṭarīq ṭuruq *road* 91

طالب → طلاب

طويل → طوال

طويل طوال ṭawīl ṭiwāl *long* 73

ظ

ظهر ẓuhr *midday* 109

ع

عادةً 9ādatan *usually* 51

عارف 9ārif *knowing* 68

عاشر 9āshir *tenth* 113

عاصمة عواصم 9āṣima 9awāṣim
capital city 92

عالم عوالم 9ālam 9awālim
world 118

عالمي 9ālamī
world(wide) 84

عامل عمّال 9āmil 9ummāl
worker, workman
50, 62, 67

عامّ 9āmm
general, public 44

عدم 9adam *lack* 95;

الرجاء عدم
ar-rajā' 9adam
please do not... 95

العراق al-9irāq *Iraq* 49

عراقي 9irāqī *Iraqi* 87

عربي → عرب

عربي عرب 9arabī 9arab
Arab 60

عشرة 9ashra *ten* 110

عقد عقود 9aqd 9uqūd

contract 99

عقد → عقود

علاقات 9alāqāt

relations 73

على 9ala *on* 52, 91

عامل → عمّال

عمان 9umān *Oman* 118

عمّان 9ammān

Amman 118

عمل أعمال 9amal a9māl

work, labour 69, 84

عن 9an *from, about* 91

عاصمة → عواصم

غ

غائب ghā'ib *absent* 84

غرب gharb *west* 44

غربي gharbī *western* 44

غير ghayr

apart from 92

ف

فبراير fibrāyir

February 115

فقير → فقراء

فقير فقراء faqīr fuqarā'

poor 50

فلسطين filasṭīn

Palestine 118

فلم أفلام film aflām *film* 59

فلوس fulūs *money* 109

فنّي fannī *technical* 48

فوراً fouran

immediately 51

فوق fouq *above, over* 92

في fī *in* 91

فيينا\ڤيينا viyēna *Vienna* 54

ق

القاهرة al-qāhira *Cairo* 49

قبل qabl *before* 91

القدس al-quds

Jerusalem 118

قراءة qirā'a

(act of) reading 73

قريب qarīb *near* 50

قسم أقسام qism aqsām

department 99

قصير → قصار

قصر قصور qaṣr quṣūr *palace* 92

قصر → قصور

قصير قصار qaṣīr qiṣār *short* 73

قطر qaṭar *Qatar* 118

قف qif *Stop!* 49, 94

قليل أقلاء qalīl aqillā'

little, few 50

قليلاً qalīlan *a little* 51

قنصلية qunṣulīya

consulate 92

ك

كـ **ka-** *like, as* 92

كاتب كتّاب **kātib kuttāb** *writer, clerk* 50, 62, 67

كامل كملة **kāmil kamala** *complete* 68

كانون الأوّل **kānūn al-'awwal** *December* 116

كانون الثاني **kānūn ath-thānī** *January* 115

كبير → كبار

كبير كبار **kabīr kibār** *big* 49

كاتب → كتّاب

كتابة **kitāba** (act of) *writing* 69

كثير **kathīr** *much* 50

كثيراً **kathīran** *greatly* 51

كراج **garāj** *garage* 91

كل **kull** *every, all* 50

كلام **kalām** *speech, speaking* 50

كمبيوتر **kampyūtir** *computer* 54

كامل → كملة

كمّية **kammīya** *quantity* 50, 55

الكويت **al-kuwayt** *Kuwait* 65, 118

كيلومتر **kīlomitr** *kilometre* 91

ل

لـ **li-** *to, for, of* 25, 91

لا **la** *no* 15

لازم **lāzim** *necessary* 67

لبنان **lubnān** *Lebanon* 14

لبناني **lubnānī** *Lebanese* 14

لتر **litr** *litre* 33

لجنة → لجان

لجنة لجان **lajna lijān** *committee* 41

لغة **lugha** *language* 73

لّما **lamma** *when* 19

لمن **li-man** *whose* 19

لون ألوان **loun alwān** *colour* 17

لي **lī** *to/for me* 14

ليبي **lībī** *Libyan* 16

ليبيا **lībiya** *Libya* 36

ليرة **līra** *lira* 33

م

مارس **māris** *March* 115

مالية **mālīya** *Financial Affairs* 99

مأمور **ma'mūr** *public official* 84

مائة **mīya** *hundred* 111

مايو **māyū** *May* 17, 115

مبلغ → مبالغ

مبروك mabrūk
Congratulations 121

مبلغ مبالغ mablagh mabāligh
sum 44

متحف ← متاحف
متّحد muttaḥid
united 68, 118

متحف متاحف mathaf matāḥif
museum 50

متر أمتار mitr amtār
metre 33

بحر ← متوسّط
مثل mithl *like, as* 19, 92
مثلاً mathalan
for example 51

مجلس ← مجالس
مجتهد mujtahid
hardworking 73

مجلس مجالس majlis majālis
council 92

مجلّة majalla
magazine 73

محاسب muḥāsib
accountant 67

محاسبات muḥāsabāt
accounts 69

محافظ muḥāfiẓ
conservative 68

محكمة ← محاكم
محامي muḥāmī *lawyer* 67

محتلّ muḥtall
occupied 118

محرّك muḥarrik
engine 50

محرّم muḥarram see 116
محفوظ maḥfūẓ *reserved* 67

محكمة محاكم maḥkama
maḥākim *law-court* 62

محلّي maḥallī *local* 73

مخرج ← مخارج
مخرج مخارج makhraj
makhārij *exit* 41, 60

مدّة مدد mudda mudad
period 109

مدخل ← مداخل
مدرسة ← مدارس
مدخل مداخل madkhal
madākhil *entrance* 41, 60

مدّة ← مدد
مدير ← مدراء
مدرّس mudarris
instructor 50, 67

مدرسة مدارس madrasa madāris
school 34, 60, 62

دفع ← مدفوعات
مدني madanī
civil, urban 84

مدير مدراء mudīr mudarā'
director 34, 60

مدينة ← مدن

مدينة مدن **madīna mudun**
city 91

مراسل **murāsil**
correspondent 73

مركز → مراكز

مربوط **marbūṭ**
connected 50

مرسل **mursil** *sender* 67;
mursal *sent* 67

مرّة **marra** *a time* 33

مريض → مرضى

مركز مراكز **markaz marākiz**
centre 92

مرور **murūr** *traffic* 33,
passing, turning 91

مريض مرضى **marīḍ marḍa**
sick 35

مساعد **musā9id**
assistant 67

مساعدة **musā9ada** *help* 69

مسافر **musāfir**
traveller 67

مستأجر **musta'jir** *tenant* 68

مستثمر **mustathmir**
investor 68

مستخدم **mustakhdim**
employer 68;
mustakhdam
employed 68

مستشفى **mustashfa**
hospital 52

مستعدّ **musta9idd**
ready 68

مستعمل **musta9mil** *user* 68

مستقبل **mustaqbil** *(radio,*
(radio, TV) receiver 68;
mustaqbal *future* 68

مستنكر **mustankar**
rejected 68

مسرور **masrūr** *pleased* 33

مسقط **masqaṭ** *Muscat* 118

مسلح **musallaḥ** *armed* 68

مسؤول **mas'ūl**
responsible 29

مشغل → مشاغل
مشكلة → مشاكل

مشترك **mushtarik**
participant 68;
mushtarak
joint, common 68

مشغل مشاغل **mashghal**
mashāghil *workshop* 50

مشغول **mashghūl**
busy 44, 67

مشكلة مشاكل **mushkila**
mashākil *problem* 50, 60

مشهور **mashhūr** *famous* 84

مصرف → مصارف
مصنع → مصانع

مصر **miṣr** *Egypt* 35

مصرف مصارف **maṣrif maṣārif**
bank 109

مصري miṣrī *Egyptian* 37

مصنع مصانع maṣna9 maṣāni9
factory 50

مطبخ → مطابخ

مطار maṭār *airport* 42

مطعم → مطاعم

مطبخ مطابخ maṭbakh
maṭābikh *kitchen* 50

مطبوع maṭbū9 *printed* 62

مطعم مطاعم maṭ9am
maṭā9im *restaurant* 44

مع ma9 *with* 91

معرض → معارض

معرض معارض ma9riḍ
ma9āriḍ *exhibition* 73

معروف ma9rūf *known* 62

معطي mu9ṭī *donor* 67

معقول ma9qūl
reasonable 84

معلم mu9allim
teacher 44, 67

معلمة mu9allima
teacher 68

معلوم ma9lūm *known* 50

معلومات ma9lūmāt
information 67

مغادرة mughādara
departure 69

المغرب al-maghrib
Morocco 118

مفتاح → مفاتيح

مفرق → مفارق

مفتاح مفاتيح miftāḥ mafātīḥ
key 50, 60

مفتّش mufattish
inspector 50, 67

مفتوح maftūḥ
open 49, 67

مفرق مفارق mafraq mafāriq
crossroad 91

مفيد mufīd *useful* 67

مقابل muqābil *facing* 68

مقالة maqāla
(press) *article* 73

مقبول maqbūl
acceptable 84

مقترح muqtaraḥ
proposed 68

مقرّر muqarrir *reporter*
50, 67; muqarrar
decided 67

مكتب\مكتبة → مكاتب

مكتب مكاتب maktab makātib
office 49, 60

مكتبة مكاتب maktaba makātib
library, bookshop 62

مكتوب maktūb
written 50, 62, 67

مكتوم maktūm
confidential 62

مكسور maksūr *broken* 68

ملابس malābis *clothes* 29

ملعب → ملاعب

مليون → ملايين

ملعب ملاعب mal9ab malā9ib
playground,
playing-field 50

ملوّن mulawwan
coloured 73

مليون ملايين milyūn malāyīn
million 111

ممتاز mumtāz
excellent 73

ممثّل mumaththil
representative 18, 67;
mumaththal
represented 67

ممرّض\ممرّضة mumarriḍ(a)
nurse 84

ممكن mumkin
possible 49

ممنوع mamnū9
prohibited 62, 67, 91

ممنون mamnūn
grateful 17

من min *from* 15, 91

مناسب munāsib
appropriate 67

مناسبة munāsaba
occasion 71

منتخب muntakhib
elector 68;
muntakhab *elected* 68

منتظر muntaẓir
waiting for 68;
muntaẓar *awaited* 68

مندوب mandūb
delegate 73

منشور manshūr
published 50

منظّمة munaẓẓama
organisation 42

مهمّ muhimm
important 67

مهندس muhandis
engineer 84

مواصلات muwāṣalāt
communications 73

موت mowt *death* 19

مؤتمر mu'tamar
conference 73

موجود moujūd
present (not absent) 84

موريتانية mūrītāniya
Mauritania 118

موظّف muwaẓẓaf
employee 84

ميلادية mīlādīya *AD* 116

مئة mīya *hundred* 111

ميدان → ميادين

ميدان ميادين maydān
mayādīn *square* 91

ن

نائب نواب nā'ib nuwwāb
deputy 62

نائم nā'im *asleep* 24

نبأ أنباء naba' anbā'
news item 24, 59

نبات nabāt *vegetation* 9

نجارة nijāra *carpentry* 62

نحن naḥnu *we* 85

نص نصوص naṣṣ nuṣūṣ *text* 73

نصف أنصاف niṣf anṣāf
half 113

نص → نصوص

نفط nafṭ *oil* 99

نقل naql *transport* 91

نقود nuqūd *money* 109

نمرة → نمر

نمرة نمر numra numar
number 99

نمل naml *ants* 16

نهائي nihā'ī *final* 27

نائب → نواب

نوفمبر nūfimbir
November 116

نيسان nīsān *April* 115

نيل nīl *Nile* 20

هـ

هامّ hāmm
important 27

هجرية hijrīya *AH* 116

هم hum *they* 27, 85

هندسة handasa
engineering 84

هندي هنود hindī hunūd
Indian 60

هندي → هنود

هو huwa *he* 27, 85

هي hiya *she* 27, 85

و

و wa *and* 17, 25

واحد wāḥid *one* 109

وارد wārid *arriving* 68

واضح wāḍiḥ *clear* 84

وراء warā' *behind* 92

وزارة wizāra *ministry* 33

وزير → وزراء

وزير وزراء wazīr wuzarā'
minister 60

وصول wuṣūl
arrival 35, 69

وطن أوطان waṭan owṭān
nation 42

وطني waṭanī *national* 42

وظيفة → وظائف

وظيفة وظائف **waẓīfa waẓā'if**
job, post 84

وقت أوقات **waqt owqāt** *time* 109

وقوف **wuqūf** *stopping* 91

وكالة **wikāla** *agency* 84

وكيل ← وكلاء

وكيل وكلاء **wakīl wukalā'**
agent 84

ي

اليابان **al-yābān** *Japan* 19

ياباني **yābānī** *Japanese* 10

يسار **yasār**
left(-hand) 91

اليمن **al-yaman**
Yemen 118

يمين **yamīn**
right(-hand) 91

يناير **yanāyir**
January 115

يهودي ← يهود

يهودي يهود **yahūdī yahūd**
Jew(ish) 60

يوليو **yūliyū** *July* 17, 115

يوم أيّام **youm ayyām**
day 17, 109;

اليوم **al-youm** *today* 99

يونيو **yūniyū** *June* 17, 115

English-Arabic Vocabulary

This vocabulary does not list:

■ the possessives, which can be found in Unit 9, the personal pronouns, which can be found in Unit 10, or the prepositions, which can be found in Unit 11,

■ numbers, days of the week or names of the months, which can all be found in Unit 13.

A

absent غائب ghā'ib 84

Abu Dhabi أبو ظبي abū ẓabī 118

academic دراسي dirāsī 37

acceptable مقبول maqbūl 84

account حساب ḥisāb 99

accountant محاسب muḥāsib 67

accounts محاسبات muḥāsabāt 69

administration إدارة idāra 34, 70

advertisement إعلان i9lān 73

aeroplane طائرة ṭā'ira 42

afternoon بعد الظهر ba9d aẓ-ẓuhr 109

agency وكالة wikāla 84

agent وكيل وكلاء wakīl wukalā' 84

agriculture زراعة zirā9a 99

air (adjective) جوّي jawwī 73

airport مطار maṭār 42

Alexandria الإسكندرية al-'iskandarīya 118

Algeria, Algiers الجزائر al-jazā'ir 118

all كلّ kull 50

a.m. صباحًا ṣabāḥan 109

ambassador سفير سفراء safīr sufarā' 48

America أميركا amayrka 61

American أميركي أميركان\ أميركيون\...يين amayrkī amayrkān/ amayrkīyūn/-īyīn 61

Amman عمّان 9ammān 118

and و wa 17, 25

announcement إعلان i9lān 73

ants نمل naml 16

appropriate مناسب munāsib 67

Arab عربي عرب 9arabī 9arab 60

armed مسلح musallaḥ 68

arrival وصول wuṣūl 35, 69

arriving وارد wārid 68	*broken* مكسور maksūr 68
(press) *article* مقالة maqāla 73	*broker* سمسار سماسير
ask for...! اطلب uṭlub 94	simsār samāsīr 84
asleep نائم nā'im 24	*bus* باص bāṣ 35;
assistant مساعد musā9id 67	أوتوبيس otobīs 54
attention اهتمام	*busy* مشغول
ihtimām 27	mashghūl 44, 67
awaited منتظر muntaẓar 68	

B

C

	Cairo القاهرة al-qāhira 49
Baghdad بغداد baghdād 118	*camels* إبل ibil 14
Bahrain البحرين	*capital city* عاصمة عواصم
al-baḥrayn 118	9āṣima 9awāṣim 92
bank بنك بنوك	*car* سيّارة sayyāra 33
bank bunūk 49, 60;	*carpentry* نجارة nijāra 62
مصرف مصارف	*Casablanca* الدّار البيضاء
maṣrif maṣārif 109	ad-dār al-bayḍā' 118
basic أساسي asāsī 37	*caution* انتباه intibāh 27
basis أساس أسس	*centre* مركز مراكز
asās usus 29	markaz marākiz 92
beautiful جميل jamīl 73	*chairman, chief* رئيس رؤساء
beginning ابتداء ibtidā' 34	ra'īs ru'asā' 33
Beirut بيروت bayrūt 118	*city* مدينة مدن
big كبير كبار	madīna mudun 91
kabīr kibār 49	*civil* مدني madanī 84
bookshop مكتبة مكاتب	*clear* واضح wāḍiḥ 84
maktaba makātib 62	*clerk* كاتب كتّاب
Britain بريطانيا	kātib kuttāb 67
barīṭāniya 42	*clothes* ملابس malābis 29
British إنجليزي إنجليز	*colleague* زميل زملاء
ingilīzī ingilīz 60	zamīl zumalā' 73

colour	لون ألوان		*country*	بلاد بلدان
	loun alwān 17			**bilād buldān** 73
coloured	ملوّن **mulawwan** 73		*crossroad*	مفرق مفارق
committee	لجنة لجان			**mafraq mafāriq** 91
	lajna lijān 41		*customs*	جمرك **jumruk** 99
common	مشترك			

D

colour لون ألوان
loun alwān 17

coloured ملوّن **mulawwan** 73

committee لجنة لجان
lajna lijān 41

common مشترك
mushtarak 68

communications مواصلات
muwāṣalāt 73

company شركة **sharika** 49

complete كامل كملة
kāmil kamala 68

computer كمبيوتر
kampyūtir 54

conference مؤتمر **mu'tamar** 73

confidential مكتوم **maktūm** 62

Congratulations مبروك
mabrūk 121

connected مربوط **marbūṭ** 50

conservative محافظ
muḥāfiẓ 68

consulate قنصلية **qunṣulīya** 92

contract عقد عقود
9aqd 9uqūd 99

correspondent مراسل
murāsil 73

cost تكليف تكاليف
taklīf takālīf 50

council مجلس مجالس
majlis majālis 92

country بلاد بلدان
bilād buldān 73

crossroad مفرق مفارق
mafraq mafāriq 91

customs جمرك **jumruk** 99

D

Damascus دمشق **dimashq** 118

danger خطر أخطار
khaṭar akhṭār 42, 59

dangerous خطر **khaṭir** 42

date تاريخ تواريخ
tārīkh tawārīkh 109

daughter بنت بنات **bint banāt** 8

day يوم أيّام
youm ayyām 17, 109

death موت **mowt** 19

decided مقرّر **muqarrar** 67

decision تقرير **taqrīr** 49, 61, 69

defence دفاع **difā9** 99

delegate مندوب **mandūb** 73

democracy دموقراطية
dimuqrāṭīya 70

department قسم أقسام
qism aqsām 99

departure مغادرة **mughādara** 69

deputy نائب نوّاب
nā'ib nuwwāb 62

despatch إرسال **irsāl** 70

difficult صعب صعاب
ṣa9b ṣi9āb 84

dinar	دينار دنانير	election	انتخاب
	dīnār danānīr 109		intikhāb 41, 70
director	مدير مدراء	elector	منتخب muntakhib 68
	mudīr mudarā' 34, 60	embassy	سفارة sifāra 48
directorate	دائرة دوائر	Emirates (United Arab)	الإمارات
	dā'ira dawā'ir 34, 99		(العربية المتّحدة)
dirham	درهم دراهم		al-'imārāt (al-9arabīya
	dirham darāhim 109		l-muttahida) 118
doctor	طبيب أطبّاء	employed	مستخدم
	tabīb atibbā' 84		mustakhdam 68
Doha	الدّوحة ad-douha 118	employee	موظّف muwazzaf 84
dollar	دولار dōlār 109	employer	مستخدم
donor	معطي mu9tī 67		mustakhdim 68
door	باب أبواب	employment	استخدام
	bāb abwāb 7		istikhdām 70
double	ثنائي thunā'ī 24	engine	محرك muharrik 50
drink!	اشرب ishrab 94	engineer	مهندس muhandis 84
driver	سائق sā'iq 50, 67	engineering	هندسة handasa 84
Dubai	دبي dubayy 118	English	إنجليزي إنجليز
			ingilīzī ingilīz 60
	E	entrance	مدخل مداخل
east	شرق sharq 49		madkhal madākhil 41, 60
economics, economy	اقتصاد	entry	دخول dukhūl 41
	iqtisād 99	every	كلّ kull 50
education	تعليم ta9līm 69;	for example	مثلاً mathalan 51
	تربية tarbiya 99	excellent	ممتاز mumtāz 73
educational	تعليمي ta9līmī 70	exchange	صرف sarf 109
Egypt	مصر misr 35	exhibition	معرض معارض
Egyptian	مصري misrī 37		ma9rid ma9ārid 73
elected	منتخب		
	muntakhab 68		

exit خروج khurūj 41;
مخرج مخارج
makhraj makhārij 41, 60

expert خبير خبراء
khabīr khubarā' 84

exploration استكشاف
istikshāf 50

F

facing مقابل muqābil 68

factory مصنع مصانع
maṣna9 maṣāni9 50

famous مشهور mashhūr 84

father أب آباء ab ābā' 7

few قليل أقلاء
qalīl aqillā' 50

film فلم أفلام
film aflām 59

final نهائي nihā'ī 27

Financial Affairs مالية
mālīya 99

financing تمويل tamwīl 17, 71

firm ثابت thābit 7

forecast تنبّؤ tanabbu' 24

foreign أجنبي أجانب
ajnabī ajānib 41, 73

Foreign Affairs خارجية
khārijīya 99

form شكل أشكال
shakl ashkāl 50, 55

foundation تأسيس ta'sīs 29

furniture أثاث athāth 7

future مستقبل mustaqbal 68

G

garage جراج\كراج garāj 91

general عام 9āmm 44

Geneva جنيف jinēv 54

gentleman سيّد سادة sayyid
sāda 34

German ألماني almānī 16

Germany ألمانيا almāniya 36

get off! انزل inzil 94

get on! اركب irkab 94

girl بنت بنات bint banāt 8

God ألله allāh 27

government حكومة ḥukūma 73

grateful ممنون mamnūn 17

greatly كثيراً kathīran 51

(Arabian) Gulf الخليج (العربي)
al-khalīj (al-9arabī) 118

H

hardworking مجتهد mujtahid 73

head رئيس رؤساء
ra'īs ru'asā' 33

help مساعدة musā9ada 69

hill تلّ تلال tall tilāl 19

Home Affairs داخلية dākhilīya 99

hospital مستشفى mustashfa 52

hotel	أوتيل ōtēl 54
hour	ساعة sā9a 109
house	بيت بيوت
	bayt buyūt 9, 60

I

immediately	فورًا fouran 51
important	هامّ hāmm 27;
	مهم muhimm 67
independence	استقلال
	istiqlāl 50, 71
Indian	هندي هنود
	hindī hunūd 60
industry	صناعة ṣinā9a 44
information	معلومات
	ma9lūmāt 67
initial	ابتدائي ibtidā'ī 37
inspection	تفتيش taftīsh 48, 69
inspector	مفتّش
	mufattish 50, 67
instruction	تدريس tadrīs 71
instructor	مدرّس
	mudarris 50, 67
insurance	تأمين ta'mīn 99
international	دولي duwalī 84
investment	استثمار istithmār 50
investor	مستثمر
	mustathmir 68
Iran	إيران īrān 33
Iranian	إيراني īrānī 36

Iraq	العراق al-9irāq 49
Iraqi	عراقي 9irāqī 87
Israel	إسرائيل isrā'īl 61
Israeli	إسرائيلي isrā'īlī 37
issue	إصدار iṣdār 73
Italian	إيطالي īṭālī 58
Italy	إيطاليا īṭāliya 42

J

Japan	اليابان al-yābān 19
Japanese	ياباني yābānī 10
Jerusalem	القدس al-quds 118
Jew(ish)	يهودي يهود
	yahūdī yahūd 60
job	شغل أشغال
	shughl ashghāl 84;
	وظيفة وظائف
	wazīfa wazā'if 84
joint	مشترك mushtarak 68
Jordan	الأردن al-'urdun 118
journalist	صحفي ṣuḥufi 73

K

key	مفتاح مفاتيح
	miftāḥ mafātīḥ 50, 60
Khartoum	الخرطوم al-khartūm 118
kilometre	كيلومتر kīlomitr 91
kitchen	مطبخ مطابخ
	matbakh matābikh 50
knowing	عارف 9ārif 68

known	معلوم ma9lūm 50; معروف ma9rūf 62	little	قليل أقلاء qalīl aqillā' 50
Kuwait	الكويت al-kuwayt 118	a little	قليلاً qalīlan 51
		local	محلّي maḥallī 73
		long	طويل طوال

L

labour	عمل أعمال 9amal a9māl 84		ṭawīl ṭiwāl 73

M

lack	عدم 9adam 95	magazine	مجلّة majalla 73
lady	سيّدة sayyida 34	mail	بريد barīd 73
language	لغة lugha 73	main	رئيسي ra'īsī 37
law-court	محكمة محاكم maḥkama maḥākim 62	market	سوق أسواق sūq aswāq (f.) 49
lawyer	محامي muḥāmī 67	Mauritania	موريتانية mūrītāniya 118
Lebanese	لبناني lubnānī 14	Mediterranean Sea	
Lebanon	لبنان lubnān 14		البحر الأبيض المتوسّط
left(-hand)	يسار yasār 91		al-baḥr al-'abyaḍ
letter	رسالة risāla 73		al-mutawassiṭ 118
library	مكتبة مكاتب maktaba makātib 62	meeting	اجتماع ijtimā9 44, 71
Libya	ليبيا lībiya 36	metre	متر أمتار mitr amtār 33
Libyan	ليبي lībī 16	midday	ظهر ẓuhr 109
licence	رخصة رخص rukhṣa rukhaṣ 99	minister	وزير وزراء wazīr wuzarā' 60
limit	حدّ حدود ḥadd ḥudūd 91	ministry	وزارة wizāra 33
line	خطّ خطوط khaṭṭ khuṭūṭ 42, 60	minute	دقيقة دقائق daqīqa daqā'iq 109
lira	ليرة līra 33	modern	حديث حداث
litre	لتر litr 33		ḥadīth ḥidāth 73

money	فلوس fulūs 109;	news item	خبر أخبار
	نقود nuqūd 109		khabar akhbār 41, 59;
money changer	صرّاف		أنباء نبأ
	ṣarrāf 109		naba' anbā' 24, 59
month	شهر أشهر	newspaper	صحيفة صحف
	shahr ashhur 33, 109		ṣaḥīfa ṣuḥuf 73;
more	أكثر akthar 50, 55		جريدة جرائد
morning	صباح ṣabāḥ 109		jarīda jarā'id 74
Morocco	المغرب	Nile	نيل nīl 20
	al-maghrib 118	no	لا la 15
Mr	سيّد سادة	north	شمال shimāl 29
	sayyid sāda 34	northern	شمالي shimālī 29
Mrs	سيّدة sayyida 34	notice	إعلان i9lān 73
much	كثير kathīr 50	now	الآن al-'ān 24
Muscat	مسقط masqaṭ 118	number	رقم أرقام
museum	متحف متاحف		raqm arqām 49;
	matḥaf matāḥif 50		نمرة نمر
			numra numar 99
N		nurse	ممرّض\ممرّضة
name	اسم اسماء		mumarriḍ(a) 84
	ism asmā' 29		
nation	وطن أوطان	**O**	
	waṭan owṭān 42	objection	احتجاج iḥtijāj 41
national	وطني waṭanī 42	occasion	مناسبة munāsaba 71
near	قريب qarīb 50	occupied	محتلّ muḥtall 118
necessary	ضروري ḍarūrī 36;	occupied territories	
	لازم lāzim 67		الأراضي المحتلّة
necessity	ضرورة ḍarūra 35		al-'arāḍī l-muḥtalla 118
new	جديد جدد	office	مكتب مكاتب
	jadīd judud 73		maktab makātib 49, 60

official	رسمي rasmī 73
officially	رسمياً rasmīyan 51
oil	نفط nafṭ 99
Oman	عمان 9umān 118
open	مفتوح maftūḥ 49, 67
open!	أفتح iftaḥ 94
or	أو ow 18
organisation	تنظيم
	tanẓīm 42, 69;
	منظّمة munaẓẓama 42

P

Pakistan	باكستان pākistān 61
palace	قصر قصور
	qaṣr quṣūr 92
Palestine	فلسطين filasṭīn 118
Paris	باريس pārīs 54
parking	إيقاف īqāf 91;
	توقيف touqīf 91
parliament	برلمان barlamān 92
participant	مشترك
	muṣtarik 68
participation	اشتراك
	iṣtirāk 70
particular	خاصّ khāṣṣ 41
partition	تقسيم taqsīm 50
passing	مرور murūr 91
payment	دفع مدفوعات
	daf9 madfū9āt 99
peace	سلام salām 93

perfect	تمام tamām 16
period	مدّة مدد
	mudda mudad 109
personal	شخصي shakhṣī 73
photograph, picture	صورة صور
	ṣūra ṣuwar 73
playground, playing-field	
	ملعب ملاعب
	mal9ab malā9ib 50
please...	الرجاء ar-rajā' 95
please do not...	الرجاء عدم
	ar-rajā' 9adam 95
pleased	مسرور masrūr 33
plumbing	سباكة sibāka 62
police	بوليس būlīs 91;
	شرطة shurṭa 42
policeman	شرطي shurṭī 92
policy, politics	سياسة siyāsa 99
poor	فقير فقراء
	faqīr fuqarā' 50
possibility	إمكانية imkānīya 50
possible	ممكن mumkin 49
post	وظيفة وظائف
	waẓīfa waẓā'if 84
pound (£)	جنيه jinayh 109
present (not absent)	
	حاضر ḥāḍir 67;
	موجود moujūd 84
presentation	تقديم taqdīm 73
president	رئيس رؤساء
	ra'īs ru'asā' 33

press	صحافة ṣiḥāfa 73
price	سعر أسعار
	si9r as9ār 44, 59
primary	ابتدائي ibtidā'ī 37
principal	رئيسي ra'īsī 37
printed	مطبوع maṭbū9 62
private	خاص khāṣṣ 41
problem	مشكلة مشاكل
	mushkila mashākil 50, 60
production	إنتاج intāj 41
professor	أستاذ أساتذة
	ustādh asātidha 34
prohibited	ممنوع
	mamnū9 62, 67, 91
proposal	اقتراح iqtirāḥ 50, 55
proposed	مقترح
	muqtaraḥ 68
public	عام 9āmm 44
public official	مأمور
	ma'mūr 84
published	منشور manshūr 50

Q

Qatar	قطر qatar 118
quantity	كمية kammīya 50, 55
question	سؤال أسئلة
	su'āl as'ila 29

R

Rabat	الرباط ar-ribāṭ 118

radio	راديو rādiō 73
reading	قراءة qirā'a 73
ready	حاضر ḥāḍir 67;
	مستعد musta9idd 68
reasonable	معقول ma9qūl 84
receiver	مستقبل
	mustaqbil 68
reception	استقبال
	istiqbāl 50, 70
recruitment	استخدام istikhdām 70
Red Sea	البحر الأحمر
	al-baḥr al-'aḥmar 118
reform	إصلاح iṣlāḥ 71
registration	تسجيل tasjīl 99
rejected	مستنكر mustankar 68
rejection	استنكار istinkār 50
relations	علاقات 9alāqāt 73
renewal	تجديد tajdīd 71
repair	تحسين taḥsīn 50
report	تقرير تقارير
	taqrīr taqārīr 49, 61, 69
reporter	مقرّر muqarrir 50, 67
representative	ممثّل
	mumaththil 18, 67
represented	ممثّل mumaththal 67
reserved	محفوظ maḥfūẓ 67
resident	ساكن سكّان
	sākin sukkān 50
responsible	مسؤول mas'ūl 29
restaurant	مطعم مطاعم
	maṭ9am maṭā9im 44

rial	ريال riyāl 33	*small*	صغير صغار	
right(-hand)	يمين yamīn 91		ṣaghīr ṣighār 50	
Riyadh	الرّياض ar-riyāḍ 118	*smoking*	تدخين tadkhīn 91	
riyal	ريال riyāl 33	*socialism*	اشتراكية	
road	طريق طرق		ishtirākīya 70	
	ṭarīq ṭuruq 91	*socialist*	اشتراكي ishtirākī 70	
Rome	روما rōma 54	*solid*	ثابت thābit 7	

son ابن أبناء ibn abnā' 8

S

		south	جنوب janūb 41
salary	راتب رواتب	*southern*	جنوبي janūbī 41
	rātib rawātib 84	*speaking*	كلام kalām 50
Saudi Arabia	السّعودية	*special*	خاصّ khāṣṣ 41
	as-sa9ūdīya 118	*specially*	خاصّةً khāṣṣatan 51
school	مدرسة مدارس	*speech*	خطاب أخطبة
	madrasa madāris 34, 60, 62		khiṭāb akhṭiba 73;
Scotland	اسكوتلندا		(= *speaking*) كلام
	iskotlanda 54		kalām 50
secondary	ثانوي thānawī 17	*speed*	سرعة sur9a 91
see...!	انظر unẓur 94	*square*	ميدان ميادين
sender	مرسل mursil 67		maydān mayādīn 91
sent	مرسل mursal 67	*Stop!*	قف qif 49, 94
sewing	خياطة khiyāṭa 62	*stopping*	وقوف wuqūf 91
short	قصيرقصار	*street*	شارع شوارع
	qaṣīr qiṣār 73		shāri9 shawāri9 44
shut!	اقفل iqfil 94	*strike*	إضراب iḍrāb 35, 70
sick	مريض مرضى	*student*	طالب طلاب
	marīḍ marḍā 35		ṭālib ṭullāb 68
sign	إشارة ishāra 91	*study*	دراسة dirāsa 34
slow down!	تمهّل	*Sudan*	السّودان
	tamahhal 27, 94		as-sūdān 118

sum	مبلغ مبالغ	
	mablagh mabāligh 44	
sun	شمس **shams** 29	
Switzerland	سويسرا **swisira** 54	
Syria	سوريا **sūriya** 36	

T

tax	ضريبة ضرائب
	ḍarība ḍarā'ib 99
tea	شاي **shāy** 29
teacher	معلم
	mu9allim 44, 67;
	معلمة **mu9allima** 68
technical	فنّي **fannī** 48
telephone	تلفون\تليفون
	tilifōn/tilīfōn 54
television	تليفزيون
	tilivizyūn 73
tenant	مستأجر **musta'jir** 68
text	نصّ نصوص
	naṣṣ nuṣūṣ 73
thing	شيء أشياء
	shay' ashyā' 29, 59
time	وقت أوقات
	waqt owqāt 109
a time	مرّة **marra** 33
today	اليوم **al-youm** 99
tools	آلات **ālāt** 15
tourism	سياحة **siyāḥa** 62
town	بلد بلاد
	balad bilād 91

town hall	بلدية **baladīya** 92
trade	تجارة **tijāra** 73
trader	تاجر تجّار
	tājir tujjār 84
traffic	مرور **murūr** 33
transfer	انتقال **intiqāl** 71
transport	نقل **naql** 91
traveller	مسافر **musāfir** 67
Tripoli	طرابلس **ṭarābulus** 118
tuition	تعليم **ta9līm** 50, 69
Tunis(ia)	تونس **tūnis** 118
turning	مرور **murūr** 91
tutorial	تعليمي **ta9līmī** 70

U

unemployment	بطالة **baṭāla** 84
united	متّحد **muttaḥid** 68, 118
university	جامعة **jāmi9a** 92
urban	مدني **madanī** 84
use	استعمال **isti9māl** 50
useful	مفيد **mufīd** 67
user	مستعمل **musta9mil** 68
usually	عادةً **9ādatan** 51

V

vegetation	نبات **nabāt** 9
Vienna	فيينا\ڤيينا **viyēna** 54
visit	زيارة **ziyāra** 33
visitor	زائر زوّار
	zā'ir zuwwār 62

voice	صوت أصوات ṣowt aṣwāt 35	worker, workman	عامل عمّال 9āmil 9ummāl 50, 62, 67

W

		workshop	مشغل مشاغل mashghal mashāghil 50
wage	أجر أجور ajr ujūr 84		
wait(ing)	انتظار intiẓār 70, 95	world	عالم عوالم 9ālam 9awālim 118
waiting for	منتظر muntaẓir 68		
warning	تنبيه tanbīh 27	world(wide)	عالمي 9ālamī 84
week	أسبوع أسابيع	writer	كاتب كتّاب kātib kuttāb 50, 62, 67
	usbū9 asābī9 44, 60		
west	غرب gharb 44	writing	كتابة kitāba 69
western	غربي gharbī 44	written	مكتوب maktūb 50, 62, 67
when	لمّا lamma 19		
where	أين ayna 11		
whose	لمن li-man 19	**Y**	
work	شغل أشغال	year	سنة سنوات sana sanawāt 29, 109
	shughl ashghāl 84;		
	عمل أعمال	Yemen	اليمن al-yaman 118
	9amal a9māl 69, 84		

INDEX

The references are to page numbers. The sign '→' refers you to an entry with references.

POCKET CARD

You may find it useful to make a pocket card from this page and carry it, for reference, when it is inconvenient to have the book with you. You can cut out the solid-line frame, fold it in half over a piece of card to stiffen it, and cover it with plastic film or heat-seal it in plastic for protection.

Alphabet

ا	alif	ف ـف	fā
ب ـب	bā	ق ـق	qāf
ت ـت	tā	ك ـك	kāf
ث ـث	thā	ل ـل	lām
ج ـج	jīm/gīm	م ـم	mīm
ح ـح	ḥā	ن ـن	nūn
خ ـخ	khā	ه ـه ـهـ هـ	hā
د ـد ذ ـذ	dāl dhāl	و	wow
ر ـر ز ـز	rā zayy	ي ـي ى	yā
س ـس ـس	sīn		
ش ـش ـش	shīn	**Variants and Signs**	
ص ـص ـص	ṣād	ء '	
ض ـض ـض	ḍād	ة	-a(t)
ط ـط ظ ـظ	ṭā ẓā	ى	-a
ع ـعـ ـغ ع	9ayn	أ ةً	-an, -atan
غ ـغـ ـغ غ	ghayn	...	(doubling)

Nouns (N) and Adjectives (A)

ة... -a(t), *f. s. (N/A); inan. pl. (A)*

ـون\ـين... -īn/-ūn, *m. an. pl. (N/A)*

ات... -āt, *f. an. pl. (N/A); inan. pl.(N)*

Command, Participles, Vb. Nouns

اكتب uktub *write!,* اشرب ishrab *drink!*

كاتب kātib *writer,* مكتوب maktūb *written*

ممثّل mumaththil *represent/ative,* -al */-ed*

مساعد musā9id *assistant*

مرسل mursil *sender,* -al *sent*

منتخب muntakhib *elect/or,* -ab */-ed*

مستخدم mustakhdim *employ/er,* -am */-ed*

تفتيش taftīsh *inspection*

مساعدة musā9ada *help*

إرسال irsāl *despatch*

أنتخاب intikhāb *election*

استخدام istikhdām *employment*

Figures (→)

٠ 0	١ 1	٢ 2	٣ 3
٤ 4	٥ 5	٦ 6	
٧ 7	٨ 8	٩ 9	